TEACHING
THE *Skills of Soccer*

900 · exerci COLLEGE LIBRARY
, SURREY KT13 8TT
79790

by
José Segura Rius

Collaborator
Carlos Sallan Macias

**Library of Congress
Cataloging Publication Data**

**Teaching the Skills of Soccer
900 Exercises and Games**
by José Segura Rius
Collaborator: Carlos Sallan Macias

Seventh Edition:
Printed in Spain by CARVIGRAfF, S. L.
Paidotribo Publishers
C/ Consejo de Ciento, 245 bis, 1st 1a
Tel 93 323 33 11-Fax. 93 453 50 33

08011 Barcelona

ISBN #1-890946-69-9
Library of Congress Control Number 2001093825
Copyright © September 2001

Editors
Javier Olivera Betran (Spanish)
Bryan R. Beaver (English)

Art Direction/Layout/Editing
Kimberly N. Bender

Drawings
Marga del Rio

Printed by
DATA REPRODUCTIONS
Auburn, Michigan

REEDSWAIN *Publishing*
612 Pughtown Road
Spring City, Pennsylvania 19475
USA
1-800-331-5191
www.reedswain.com
EMAIL:info@reedswain.com

TEACHING
THE *Skills of Soccer*

900+ exercises and games

by
José Segura Rius

Collaborator
Carlos Sallan Macias

7th Edition

published by
REEDSWAIN *Publishing*

TABLE OF CONTENTS

INTRODUCTION

When I began to think about the content of this book, I had only two clear ideas: one was that this would be a work about all the different technical elements that form what we know as soccer technique, and the other was that it must at the same time be extensive, varied, and a source of information for all those people (coaches, fitness trainers and Physical Education professors) who as I, move, work, and love this world of physical activity and sports and especially Soccer.

The objective of this book is to be able to use a combination of exercises and games genuinely based on sound soccer techniques.

With the passage of time, when I was mentally situated within the very content of the book, and I had already overcome the first feelings of doubt about the use and importance that the work that I was to do could have, I wanted to include those personal concerns, those criteria about how one ought to structure and on what foundation ought to rest the learning of the different technical elements in different sports and especially Soccer.

The first step was the realization of a deep analysis about the aspects that are immersed in the core of any technical performance and that they affect, by their involvement, the development of this.

Each one of the technical gestures peculiar to soccer has been developed under the same criteria:1st- application plays for each technical element and 2nd-specific exercises for each one of the factors that influence the correct performance of the movement, with gradual difficulty, established according to pedagogical criteria and based on the difficulty peculiar to the exercise and on the technical demand that the exercise could require.

The result has formed a combination of activities applied to soccer so that all those who need it: trainers, Physical Education professors, etc. can have recourse to collecting information and be able to plant not only the teaching of different technical elements, directed toward those factors that influence its performance, but also the correction of those parts of the movement that the student-player performs incorrectly and that they can be worked on partially to improve them successfully.

This book proposes to give information that has a double meaning, on one side to be a source of information for all those looking for a variety of exercises and plays for their class or training sessions and on the other, to indicate the way to influence the different factors which optimize the technical gesture and above all its correction.

The treatment given to each one of the technical elements is basically the same, and as such has been commented previously; I have tried to cover a wide fan of possibilities that interest not only lovers of analytical teaching methods, but also those who work only with globalized teaching methods.

This work does not try to be a methodological process that one must follow for the teaching and the learning of the technique of soccer, it doesn't pretend this. I have tried only to give a wide, voluminous and specific base of exercises, complementary activities and application plays about the different technical elements of soccer.

However, the combination of exercises gathered in this work do not serve only to improve the performance of technical gestures (which ultimately influence the correct performance of the technique and the tactic of soccer, but also can be directed, although as a secondary objective, to improve all those physical qualities that intervene in soccer (you will find exercises which also improve resistance, speed, strength...).

At the same time, many exercises are focused on the improvement of the will (desire), an essential factor in the player's behavior before the learning situation can significantly improve a concrete action. Systematic repetition of the exercises shown here aren't useful unless an attitude (the will) exists to want to improve and to assimilate new levels of performance that will benefit not only the player but also the team. Repetition of the exercises or application plays is not only limited to runs, sprints, strikes, head strikes, dribbles , etc.; but rather to the analysis of the play situation and paying attention to each one of the movements that each player is to develop. Each player must know why he makes each action and how he does it.

Each one of the exercises represented in this work is done in what we understand as general conditions and that at no time do they mean to be the only way, but rather complete liberty is left to all those responsible for the training sessions or classes so that they adapt to the characteristics of the players, playing field dimensions, number of repetitions, distances of passes, etc.

At the same time, we have developed a kind of scorecard that could be flexible, inclusive and efficient for all those who review it. Each exercise is given a Difficulty rating which represents the physical and technical demand on the players (1- minimal difficulty, 2 -moderate difficulty, 3-high moderate difficulty, 4- maximum difficulty), the material needed, the minimal number of players that are required for the optimal realization of the exercise and lastly the description and graphic representation of the exercise.

This work is born from the hand of a professional lover of soccer who only tries to go into depths about this passionate sport and who is open to all those suggestions, criteria and commentaries that in themselves can be done, taking for granted that behind each one of them the contents here explained will be able to be perfected; and doubtless one will be able to continue improving and learning constantly.

I welcome all the suggestions that you would forward since it is always very important, enriching and necessary to be able to learn form others.

José Segura Rius

CHAPTER 1
INDIVIDUAL EXERCISES

Objective: Control of the ball
Difficulty: 2
No. of players: One
Material: One ball per player
Description: The player makes the greatest number of possible touches, not letting the ball touch the ground, hitting it with his foot.

Objective: Control of the ball
Difficulty: 2
No. of players: One
Material: One ball per player
Description: The player makes the greatest number of possible touches, not letting the ball fall to the ground, striking it with one foot then the other.

Objective: Control of the ball
Difficulty: 2
No. of players: One
Material: One ball per player
Description: The player makes the greatest number of possible touches, not letting the ball fall to the ground, striking it with one foot. He changes to the other foot when the coach signals.

Objective: Control of the ball
Difficulty: 2
No. of players: One
Material: One ball per player
Description: The player makes the greatest number of possible touches, not letting the ball fall to the ground, hitting it with his thigh.

Objective: Control of the ball
Difficulty: 2
No. of players: One
Material: One ball per player
Description: The player makes the greatest number of possible touches, not letting the ball fall to the ground, striking it with each thigh alternately.

Objective: Control of the ball
Difficulty: 2
No. of players: One
Material: One ball per player
Description: The player strikes the ball repeatedly against the wall, not letting it fall to the ground. He can use any body surface.

Objective: Control of the ball
Difficulty: 2
No. of players: One
Material: One ball per player
Description: The player makes the greatest number of touches possible with his head, not letting the ball fall to the ground.

Objective: Control of the ball
Difficulty: 2
No. of players: One
Material: One ball per player
Description: The player makes touches with his head, not letting the ball fall to the ground. At the coach's signal, the player makes a thigh touch.

Objective: Control of the ball
Difficulty: 2
No. of players: One
Material: One ball per player
Description: The player makes the greatest possible number of touches, not letting the ball fall to the ground, using different touch surfaces according to the following sequence: foot, thigh, head, foot…from the same side.

Objective: Control of the ball
Difficulty: 2
No. of players: One
Material: One ball per player
Description: The player makes the greatest possible number of touches, not letting the ball fall to the ground, using different touch surfaces according to the following sequence: right foot, left foot, right thigh, left thigh, head, right foot, left foot.

Objective: Control of the ball
Difficulty: 2
No. of players: One
Material: One ball per player
Description: The player makes the greatest possible number of touches, not letting the ball fall to the ground, using different contact surfaces according to the following sequence: foot, thigh, head, thigh, foot, thigh, head.

Objective: Control of the ball
Difficulty: 2
No. of players: One
Material: One ball per player
Description: The player makes the greatest possible number of touches, not letting the ball fall to the ground, using different contact surfaces according to the following sequence: right-left foot, right-left thigh, head, right-left thigh…

Objective: Control of the ball
Difficulty: 2
No. of players: One
Material: One ball per player
Description: The player makes the greatest possible number of touches, not letting the ball fall to the ground, using different contact surfaces according to the following sequence: right-left foot, right-left thigh, head, right –left foot. Here, instead of making just one touch with each surface, the player makes two or three before changing.

Objective: Control of the ball
Difficulty: 2
No. of players: One
Material: One ball per player
Description: The player makes the greatest possible number of touches, not letting the ball fall to the ground, using different surface contacts according to the sequence: foot, thigh, head, thigh, foot...Again, instead of one touch several are made before changing the contact surface.

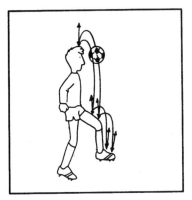

Objective: Control of the ball
Difficulty: 2
No. of players: One
Material: One ball per player
Description: The player juggles with any part of the body, not letting the ball fall to the ground. At the coach's signal, the player must change the contact surface.

Objective: Control of the ball
Difficulty: 2
No. of players: One
Material: One ball per player
Description: The player juggles with a specific body surface, not letting the ball fall to the ground, while moving about the playing field.

Objective: Control of the ball
Difficulty: 3
No. of players: One
Material: One ball per player
Description: The player juggles with a specific body surface, not letting the ball fall to the ground, while he is moving about the field of play. When he arrives at the "net" he makes a higher touch so that the ball passes over and he continues on the other side.

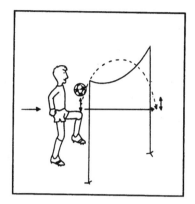

Objective: Control of the ball
Difficulty: 3
No. of players: One
Material: One ball per player and 5-6 cones
Description: The player juggles with a specific body surface, not letting the ball fall to the ground, while he moves in a slalom through the cones.

Objective: Control of the ball
Difficulty: 3
No. of players: One
Material: One ball per player and 6-8 cones.
Description: The player juggles with a specific body surface, not letting the ball fall to the ground while moving in a straight line through the path marked off by the cones.

Objective: Control of the ball
Difficulty: 3
No. of players: One
Material: One ball per player and 4- 6 cones
Description: The player juggles with a specific body surface, not letting the ball fall to the ground, while moving in the direction marked off by the cones.

Objective: Control of the ball
Difficulty: 3
No. of players: One
Material: One ball per player and 2-3 low benches.
Description: The player juggles with a specific body surface, not letting the ball fall to the ground, while he moves throughout the field. When he arrives in front of a bench he must try to send the ball over it without losing control.

Objective: Control of the ball
Difficulty: 3
No. of players: One
Material: One ball per player and 5-6 cones
Description: The player juggles with a specific body surface, not letting the ball fall to the ground, while he moves about the field in a zig-zag formation, following the path set out by cones.

Objective: Control of the ball
Difficulty: 3
No. of players: One
Material: One ball per player
Description: The player juggles with a specific body surface, not letting the ball fall to the ground, while he moves backwards throughout the field of play.

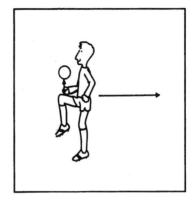

Objective: Control of the ball
Difficulty: 4
No. of players: One
Material: One ball per player
Description: The player juggles with a specific body surface, not letting the ball fall to the ground. At the coach's signal, the player makes a high touch, sits on the ground and gets up again to continue juggling.

Objective: Control of the ball
Difficulty: 4
No. of players: One
Material: One ball per player
Description: The player juggles with a specific body surface, not letting the ball fall to the ground. At the coach's signal, the player makes a high touch, turns 360 degrees on his body's longitudinal axis and continues juggling.

Objective: Control of the ball
Difficulty: 4
No. of players: One
Material: One ball per player
Description: The player juggles with a specific body surface, not letting the ball fall to the ground. At the coach's signal, the player makes a high touch, turns 360 degrees on his body's transversal axis (rolls over) and continues juggling.

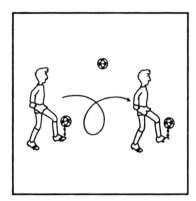

Objective: Control of the ball
Difficulty: 4
No. of players: One
Material: One ball per player
Description: The player juggles with a specific body surface, not letting the ball fall to the ground. At the coach's signal, he sends the ball back over his head, makes a half turn and continues juggling.

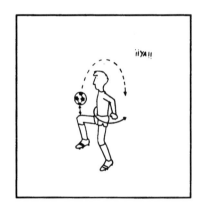

Objective: Control of the ball
Difficulty: 2
No. of players: One
Material: One ball per player
Description: The player holds the ball between his feet and moves by jumping throughout the field of play.

Objective: Control of the ball
Difficulty: 3
No. of players: 2
Material: One ball per pair
Description: Players make two touches with their feet and pass the ball to their teammate, not letting the ball fall to the ground at any time.

Objective: Control of the ball
Difficulty: 3
No. of players: 2
Material: One ball per pair
Description: Players make two touches with their thighs and pass the ball to the teammate, not letting the ball fall to the ground at any time.

Objective: Control of the ball
Difficulty: 3
No. of players: 2
Material: One ball per pair
Description: Players make two touches with their heads and pass the ball to their teammate, not letting the ball fall to the ground at any time.

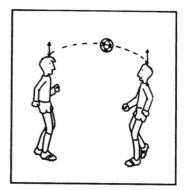

Objective: Control of the ball
Difficulty: 3
No. of players: 2
Material: One ball per pair
Description: Players make a touch with each body surface and pass the ball to their teammate, not letting the ball fall to the ground at any time, following the order established: foot, thigh, head, pass, head, thigh, foot, thigh.

Objective: Control of the ball
Difficulty: 3
No. of players: 2
Material: One ball per pair
Description: Players make a touch with each body surface and pass the ball to their teammate, not letting the ball fall to the ground at any time, following the order established. Here we see: head, thigh, foot, pass, foot, thigh, head, thigh.

Objective: Control of the ball
Difficulty: 3
No. of players: 2
Material: One ball per pair
Description: One of the players is making a touch with a specific surface, not letting the ball fall to the ground. At the coach's signal, the player passes the ball to his teammate who continues juggling with the same contact surface.

Objective: Control of the ball
Difficulty: 3
No. of players: 2
Material: One ball per pair
Description: The players move side by side through space, passing the ball after making 2-3 touches.

Objective: Control of the ball
Difficulty: 3
No. of players: 2
Material: One ball per pair
Description: Players move forward side by side, passing the ball after making 2-3 touches.

Objective: Control of the ball
Difficulty: 3
No. of players: 2
Material: One ball pair
Description: Players move throughout the playing area, one behind the other. The one who is behind makes 2-3 touches and makes a pass over his teammate's head, who controls and repeats the same action to the first player who has moved to the front.

Objective: Control of the ball
Difficulty: 3
No. of players: 2
Material: One ball per pair and 1 cone
Description: Player A juggles with a specific surface, not letting the ball fall to the ground, circles the cone and returns to give the ball to player B, who does the same.

Objective: Control of the ball
Difficulty: 3
No. of players: 2
Material: One ball per player and 4 cones
Description: Players are juggling, not letting the ball fall to the ground, while they move around the cones and try to catch each other.

Objective: Control of the ball
Difficulty: 3
No. of players: 2
Material: One ball per player and 4 cones
Description: Players are juggling, not letting the ball fall to the ground, while moving back and forth between two cones as in the diagram.

Objective: Control of the ball
Difficulty: 3
No. of players: 2
Material: One ball per player, 12 cones.
Description: Each player juggles with a specific surface, not letting the ball fall to the ground, without going out of his square. At the coach's signal they exchange positions without leaving the pathway or letting the ball fall to the ground.

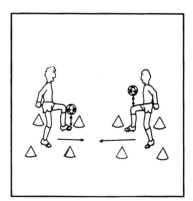

Objective: Control of the ball
Difficulty: 3
No. of players: 2
Material: One ball per player
Description: The two players juggle with a specific surface, not letting the ball fall to the ground. At the coach's signal they exchange balls and continue juggling.

Objective: Control of the ball
Difficulty: 3
No. of players: 2
Material: One ball per player, 12 cones.
Description: A makes 2-3 touches with a specific surface and passes the ball to B who makes 2-3 touches with the same surface. Then he returns the ball to A to repeat the exercise with another contact surface.

Objective: Control of the ball
Difficulty: 3
No. of players: Groups of 2
Material: One ball per group
Description: Player A throws the ball in the air and leapfrogs over his teammate B to control the ball with his foot before it hits the ground.

Objective: Control of the ball
Difficulty: 3
No. of players: Groups of 2
Material: One ball per group
Description: Player A throws the ball in the air and leapfrogs over his teammate B, to control the ball with his head and then with his foot without letting it touch the ground.

Exercises in groups of 3

Objective: Control of the ball
Difficulty: 3
No. of players: 3
Material: One ball per group
Description: Players, positioned in a triangular formation, pass the ball after making two touches with the foot, not letting the ball touch the ground.

Objective: Control of the ball
Difficulty: 3
No. of players: 3
Material: One ball per group
Description: Players, positioned in a triangular formation, pass the ball after making two touches with the thigh, not letting the ball touch the ground.

Objective: Control of the ball
Difficulty: 3
No. of players: 3
Material: One ball per group
Description: Players, positioned in a triangular formation, pass the ball after making two touches with the head, not letting the ball touch the ground.

Objective: Control of the ball
Difficulty: 3
No. of players: 3
Material: One ball per group
Description: Players, positioned in a triangular formation, pass the ball after making a touch with each foot, not letting the ball touch the ground.

Objective: Control of the ball
Difficulty: 3
No. of players: 3
Material: One ball per group
Description: Players, positioned in a triangular formation, pass the ball after making a touch with each thigh, not letting the ball fall to the ground.

Objective: Control of the ball
Difficulty: 3
No. of players: 3
Material: One ball per player and 3 cones
Description: Players, positioned in a triangular formation, each one next to a cone, are juggling with a specific surface, not letting the ball fall to the ground. At a signal from the coach, each player moves toward the cone to his left, continuing to juggle.

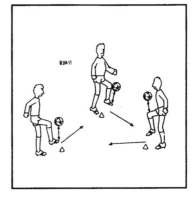

Objective: Control of the ball
Difficulty: 3
No of players: 3
Material: One ball per player and 2 cones
Description: Players are located as the diagram indicates.
The first player juggles the ball up to the cone in front of him and gives the ball to that player who juggles to the third cone and gives the ball to the third player and the exercise continues.

Objective: Control of the ball
Difficulty: 3
No. of players: 3
Material: One ball per group
Description: Player A makes 2-3 touches with a specific surface and makes a pass to player B who, after controlling the ball, turns and makes a pass to player C, who repeats the same action as player A.

Objective: Control of the ball
Difficulty: 3
No. of players: 3
Material: One ball per player and 3 cones
Description: Players are located as the diagram indicates. Each one juggles on a specific surface, next to his cone, not letting the ball fall to the ground. At the coach's signal each player moves to the cone on his left, continuing to juggle.

Objective: Control of the ball
Difficulty: 3
No. of players: 3
Material: One ball per player and 4 cones
Description: Players are positioned as indicated in the diagram. Each one juggles with a specific surface, next to a cone, not letting the ball fall to the ground. At the coach's signal each player circles the center cone and returns to his position, continuing to juggle.

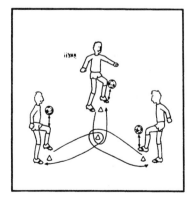

Objective: Control of the ball
Difficulty: 3
No. of players: 3
Material: One ball per player
Description: Players are positioned as indicated in the diagram. They each juggle with a specific surface, not letting the ball fall to the ground. At the coach's signal each player passes the ball to the player to his left to continue juggling.

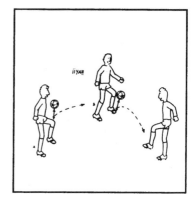

Objective: Control of the ball
Difficulty: 3
No. of players: 3
Material: Two balls per group
Description: Players are positioned as indicated in the diagram. Players A and B juggle with a specific surface, not letting the ball fall to the ground and pass the ball alternately to player C, who returns the ball after making 2-3 touches.

Objective: Control of the ball
Difficulty: 4
No. of players: 3
Material: Two balls per group
Description: Players move through the space as the diagram indicates. Players A and B juggle with a specific surface, not letting the ball fall to the ground and pass the ball alternately to player C who returns it after making 2-3 touches.

Objective: Control of the ball
Difficulty: 4
No. of players: 3
Material: Two balls per group
Description: Players move throughout the space as the diagram indicates. Players A and B juggle with a specific surface, not letting the ball fall to the ground and pass it alternately to player C who returns it after making 2-3 touches.

Objective: Control of the ball
Difficulty: 3
No. of players: 3
Material: One ball per group
Description: Players are positioned as the diagram indicates. Player A juggles with a specific surface, not letting the ball fall to the ground, while he moves between his teammates in a figure 8 formation.

Objective: Control of the ball
Difficulty: 3
No. of players: 3
Material: One ball per player and 3 cones
Description: Players are positioned as the diagram indicates. Each player juggles according to the cone he is playing (ex. Cone A=thigh, Cone B=head . . .). At the coach's signal, the players go toward the cone on their left juggling with the same surface; when they arrive at the cone they change to the contact surface corresponding to that cone.

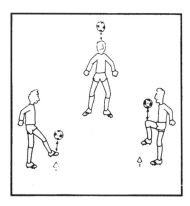

Exercises in groups of 4

Objective: Control of the ball
Difficulty: 3
No. of players: 4
Material: 3 balls per group
Description: Players A, B, C juggle with a specific surface, not letting ball fall to the ground; they pass it alternately to player D who makes 2-3 touches and returns the ball to the player who passed it to him.

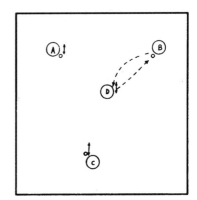

Objective: Control of the ball
Difficulty: 3
No. of players: 4
Material: Two balls per group
Description: Players are positioned as the diagram indicates. Players A and B juggle with a specific surface, not letting the ball fall to the ground; at the signal they pass to players C and D, respectively, who turn while juggling to pass the ball again to B and A.

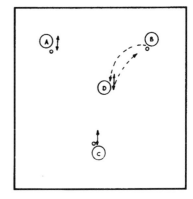

Objective: Control of the ball
Difficulty: 3
No. of players: 4
Material: 4 balls and 4 cones per group
Description: Players are positioned as the diagram indicates, each one next to his cone, make touches with a specific surface, not letting the ball fall to the ground. At the signal they go toward the cone located at their right, continuing to juggle.

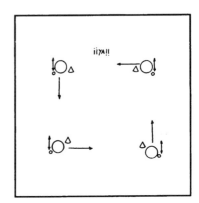

Objective: Control of the ball
Difficulty: 3
No. of players: 4
Material: 4 balls and 4 cones per group
Description: Players are positioned as the diagram indicates, each one next to his cone, and juggle with a specific surface, not letting the ball fall to the ground. At the signal they go toward the cone located on their diagonal , continuing to juggle.

Objective: Control of the ball
Difficulty: 3
No. of players: 4
Material: 3 balls and 4 cones per group
Description: Players are positioned as the diagram indicates, each one next to his cone, and juggle with a specific surface, not letting the ball fall to the ground. At the signal they pass to the player to their right and turn to receive the pass from the player on their left, continuing to juggle.

Objective: Control of the ball
Difficulty: 3
No. of players: 4
Material: 4 balls and 5 cones per group
Description: Players are positioned as the diagram indicates, each one next to his cone, and make touches with a specific surface, not letting the ball fall to the ground. At the signal they circle the center cone, continuing to juggle and return to the starting point.

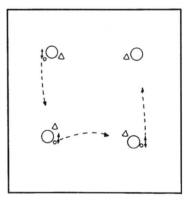

Objective: Control of the ball
Difficulty: 3
No. of players: 4
Material: 4 balls and 5 cones per group
Description: Players are positioned as the diagram indicates, each one next to his cone, and juggle with a specific surface, not letting the ball fall to the ground. At the signal they circle the center cone, continuing to juggle and go to the opposite cone.

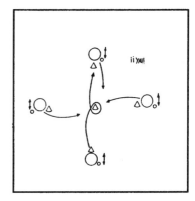

Objective: Control of the ball
Difficulty: 3
No. of players: 4
Material: 4 balls and 5 cones per group
Description: Players are positioned as the diagram indicates, each one next to his cone, and make touches with a specific surface, not letting the ball fall to the ground. At the signal they circle the center cone, continuing to juggle, and go to the cone on their right.

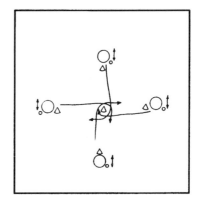

Objective: Control of the ball
Difficulty: 4
No. of players: 4
Material: 4 balls and 8 cones per group
Description: Players are positioned as the diagram indicates; they juggle with a specific surface, not letting the ball fall to the ground. At the signal they leave the square and go toward any cone, continuing to juggle.

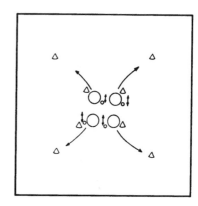

Objective: Control of the ball
Difficulty: 3
No. of players: 4
Material: One ball and two cones per group
Description: Players are positioned as the diagram indicates. The first player juggles with a specific surface, not letting the ball fall to the ground, while he moves toward the cone in front of him and gives the ball to the next player who does the same in the opposite direction.

Objective: Control of the ball
Difficulty: 3
No. of players: 4
Material: One ball per group
Description: Players are positioned as the diagram indicates. The first player juggles with a specific surface, not letting the ball fall to the ground, while he moves in slalom formation among his teammates. When he arrives at the starting point he makes a pass to the other end to his teammate who repeats the exercise.

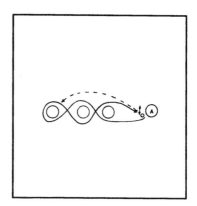

Exercises in various groups

Objective: Control of the ball
Difficulty: 3
No. of players: Various groups
Material: One ball per player
Description: Players, divided in two groups, are positioned at the ends of the field. At the signal they move toward the opposite end while juggling with a specific surface, not letting the ball fall to the ground. This is especially difficult in the center of the field when the two groups pass by one another.

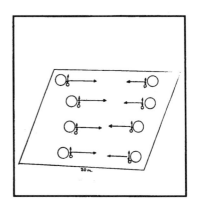

Objective: Control of the ball
Difficulty: 3
No. of players: Various groups
Material: One ball per player
Description: The players, placed freely through-out the field of play, juggle with a specific surface, not letting the ball fall to the ground. The objective is to be the last player to lose control of the ball.

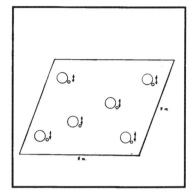

Objective: Control of the ball
Difficulty: 2
No. of players: Various groups
Material: One ball per player and 9 cones
Description: Each player juggles with a specific surface, not letting the ball fall to the ground, while circling each one of the outside cones after circling the center cone.

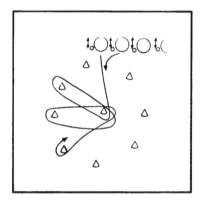

Objective: Control of the ball
Difficulty: 2
No. of players: Various groups
Material: One ball per group
Description: The ball must make several round trips in such a way that each player makes 2-3 touches and passes the ball as the diagram shows.
Round trip no. 1. Touches with the foot.
Round trip no. 2. Touches with the thigh.
Round trip no. 3. Touches with the head.

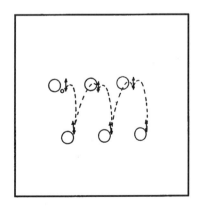

Objective: Control of the ball
Difficulty: 3
No. of players: Various groups
Material: One ball per player and 4 cones
Description: Players make free touches in the space set out by cones. Each player has a letter and each cone a number. The coach will call out a letter and a number so that the named player goes toward the corresponding cone before his teammates can stop him.

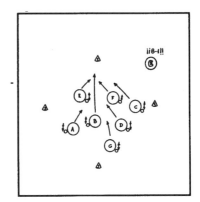

Objective: Control of the ball
Difficulty: 3
No. of players: Various groups
Material: One ball per player and 10 cones
Description: Players A and B move in a zig-zag formation among the cones, as the diagram indicates, while they juggle with a specific surface, not letting the ball fall to the ground. When they arrive at the end they give the ball to the next player in line.

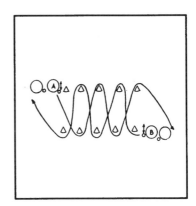

Objective: Control of the ball
Difficulty: 3
No. of players: Various groups
Material: One ball and two cones per group.
Description: The players try to make exchange runs following the course the diagram indicates, juggling with any surface and not letting the ball fall to the ground.

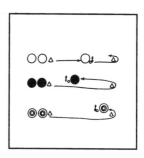

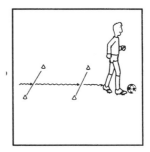

CHAPTER 2
DRIBBLING THE BALL
Dribbling with different surface touches

Objective: Dribbling - Surface touches
Difficulty: 2
No. of players: One
Material: One ball per player
Description: The player dribbles the ball through the path formed by the cones; when the player reaches each cone, he must stop the ball with the sole of the foot and continue dribbling up to the other cones.

Objective: Dribbling - Surface touches
Difficulty: 2
No. of players: One
Material: One ball per player
Description: Player A dribbles the ball and at the coach's signal, must change direction with the medial part of the foot.

Objective: Dribbling - Surface touches.
Difficulty: 2
No. of players: One
Material: One ball per player
Description: Player A dribbles the ball backward by means of successive touches with the sole of the foot.

Objective: Dribbling - Surface touches.
Difficulty: 3
No. of players: One
Material: One ball per player
Description: Player A dribbles the ball sideways with successive touches with the medial part of the foot in the opposite direction.

Objective: Dribbling - Surface touches.
Difficulty: 3
No. of players: One
Material: One ball per player
Description: Player A dribbles the ball sideways with successive touches with the lateral part of the foot.

Objective: Dribbling - Surface touches.
Difficulty: 3
No. of players: One
Material: One ball per player
Description: The player dribbles the ball with changes of direction made with the sole of the foot.

Objective: Dribbling - Surface touches.
Difficulty: 3
No. of players: One.
Material: One ball per player
Description: The player dribbles the ball in a straight line with successive touches with the two medial parts of each foot.

Objective: Dribbling - Surface touches.
Difficulty: 3
No. of players: One
Material: One ball per player
Description: The player dribbles the ball rapidly in a straight line with the instep.

Objective: Dribbling - Surface touches.
Difficulty: 3
No. of players: Various groups
Material: One ball per player
Description: Players placed in two groups exchange the ball while dribbling. When they arrive at the other group they place themselves at the end of the line. They work different touch surfaces.

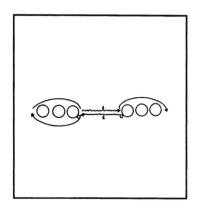

Objective: Dribbling - Surface touches.
Difficulty: 3
No. of players: Various groups
Material: Two balls and one cone per group
Description: Players are distributed into four groups. Each player who has a ball when he arrives at the cone turns to his left. When they finish dribbling they stay in the same group. Players should work different body contact surfaces.

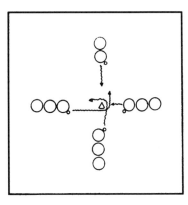

Objective: Dribbling - Surface touches.
Difficulty: 3
No. of players: Various groups
Material: Two balls per group
Description: Players are placed in four groups. Dribbling between A and B will be done with the lateral part of the foot and the dribbling between C and D with the medial part of the foot. When they finish dribbling they go to the adjacent group.

Objective: Dribbling - Surface touches.
Difficulty: 3
No. of players: Groups of 2
Material: One ball per group
Description: Player A dribbles the ball in a straight line. Every 3-4 steps he steps on the ball with the sole of his foot and leaves it to his teammate B who runs behind him. B gets the ball and dribbles it past player A to repeat the exercise.

Dribbling - straight trajectory

Objective: Straight trajectory
Difficulty: 1
No. of players: Groups of 4-5
Material: Two balls and one hoop per group
Description: Each team has two balls. One ball is located on the exit line and the other ball is inside of the hoop 10 yards away. At the signal a player dribbles up to the hoop to switch balls, turns and dribbles back to the exit line.

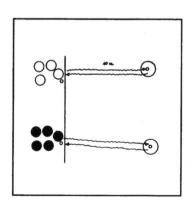

Objective: Straight trajectory
Difficulty: 1
No. of players: Groups of 2
Material: Two balls per group
Description: Two players dribble straight ahead through the field while maintaining a conversation.

Objective: Straight trajectory
Difficulty: 1
No. of players: One
Material: One ball per player
Description: Each player dribbles his ball and after 5-6 passes makes a long dribble, sprints to regain it and continues dribbling.

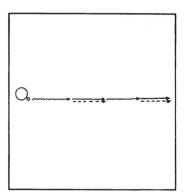

Objective: Straight-line trajectory
Difficulty: 3
No. of players: One
Material: One ball per player
Description: Each player dribbles the ball and after 5-6 passes makes a longer touch to regain it after performing a somersault.

Objective: Straight-line trajectory
Difficulty: 3
No. of players: Groups of three
Material: One ball and two cones per group
Description: Player A dribbles the ball up to the cone where he meets teammate C. From there he throws the ball so that C goes after it, controls it and dribbles it up to B who begins the exercise again.

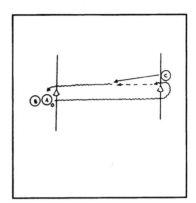

Objective: Straight-line trajectory
Difficulty: 3
No. of players: Groups of three
Material: One ball and two cones per group
Description: Player A dribbles the ball towards player C at the opposite cone. Halfway there, he passes the ball to C who returns it to him with the first touch and he continues dribbling until arriving at the cone, where he passes to C. Player C then dribbles until arriving at the opposite cone.

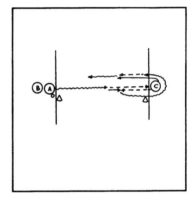

Objective: Straight-line trajectory
Difficulty: 2
No. of players: Groups of 4-5
Material: 2-3 balls per group and four cones
Description: Player A dribbles up to the cone where he finds teammate C, to whom he passes the ball. C dribbles toward the next cone, and does the same maneuver with D, etc. The players remain at the cones until they get the ball again.

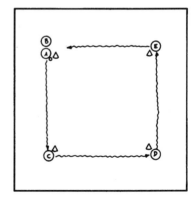

Objective: Straight-line trajectory
Difficulty: 8
No. of players: Groups of 10-12
Material: 4-5 balls and 4 cones
Description: This is similar to the previous exercise but with two players per cone. Player A dribbles counter-clockwise toward D, while B dribbles clockwise toward H. There they will give up the ball and will wait to be relieved.

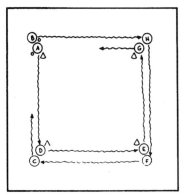

Objective: Straight-line trajectory
Difficulty: 2
No. of players: Groups of 4-5
Material: 2-3 balls and 4 cones
Description: All players dribble the ball toward the first cone, make a complete turn, and continue toward the next one, where they repeat the same movement, then on to the next and so on.

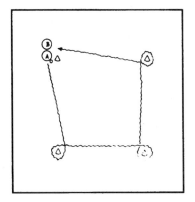

Objective: Straight-line trajectory
Difficulty: 2
No. of players: Groups of 5-6
Material: 4-5 balls and 5 cones
Description: Similar to the previous exercise, with one change: all players are to pass by the center cone and make a complete turn.

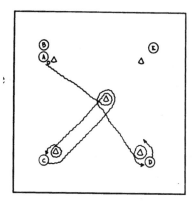

Objective: Straight-line trajectory
Difficulty: 2
No. of players: Groups of 5-6
Material: 4 balls and 3 cones
Description: All players leave their respective cones and go toward the central cone; they make a complete turn and go toward the opposing cone.

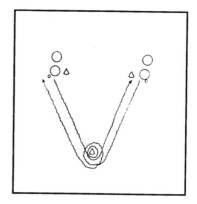

Objective: Straight-line trajectory
Difficulty: 2
No. of players: Groups of 5-6
Material: 4 balls and 3 cones
Description: Exercise is similar to the last one with one variation: when they arrive at the center cone they make a complete turn and return to their original cone.

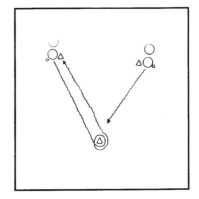

Objective: Straight-line trajectory
Difficulty: 3
No. of players: Groups of 5-6
Material: 4-5 balls and 7 cones
Description: Distribution: 5 cones in a row plus a pivot cone. Players move away from cone 1 in the direction of the pivot cone, circle it and go to cone 2. After a turn around each cone they go toward the pivot cone. When they arrive at cone 5 they continue in the opposite direction (cone 4, cone 3, cone 2, cone 1). This exercise can be done by two groups simultaneously with one starting at cone 1 and the other at cone 5.

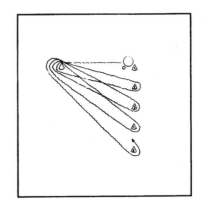

Objective: Straight-line trajectory
Difficulty: 2
No. of players: Groups of 8-10
Material: 4 balls and 8 cones
Description: Each group dribbles the ball toward their respective cone, circles it and returns.

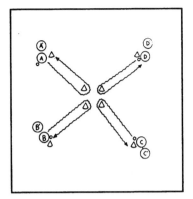

Objective: Straight-line trajectory
Difficulty: 3
No. of players: Groups of 6-8
Material: Two balls and 8 cones
Description: Players A and B dribble toward their teammates C and D, making a complete revolution at all the cones. Players C and D repeat the exercise.

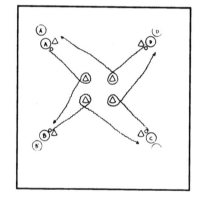

Objective: Straight-line trajectory
Difficulty: 2
No. of players: Groups of 3-4
Material: Two balls and 3 cones per group
Description: Players A and B dribble the ball around the cones as in the diagram and pass off to the next in line to repeat the exercise.

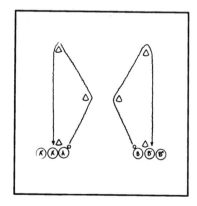

Objective: Straight-line trajectory
Difficulty: 2
No. of players: Groups of 4
Material: Two balls per group
Description: Players A and B dribble the ball toward their teammates C and D, who are running toward them, execute a quick give-and-go as they pass by and continue dribbling.

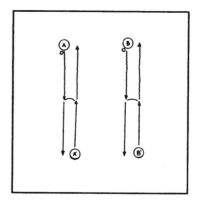

Objective: Straight-line trajectory
Difficulty: 3
No. of players: Groups of 6-8
Material: Two balls and 4 cones
Description: Players A and B dribble the ball toward the opposing cone to circle it and return to the starting point. The teams play as in a relay race.

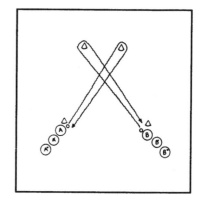

Objective: Straight-line trajectory
Difficulty: 3
No. of players: One
Material: One ball per player
Description: The player dribbles in a straight line. At the coach's signal, he makes a change of direction.

Objective: Straight-line trajectory
Difficulty: 3
No. of players: Groups of 2
Material: One ball per player
Description: Free dribbling through the field in a straight line, the first player leads while the second follows.

Objective: Straight-line trajectory
Difficulty: 4
No. of players: Groups of 2
Material: One ball per player
Description: The players form pairs, each player has a number 1 or 2 assigned. The coach says a number and this player becomes the "chaser".

Objective: Straight-line trajectory
Difficulty: 3
No. of players: Any number
Material: One ball per player
Description: Each player dribbles his ball while watching the coach, who signals different numbers with a raised arm which the players must shout out.

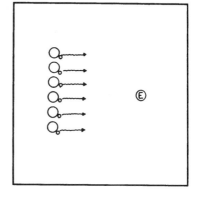

Objective: Straight-line trajectory
Difficulty: 4
No. of players: Groups of 2
Material: One ball per pair and 6-8 cones
Description: Player B dribbles the ball toward the first cone; when he arrives there he passes toward A who has moved to receive. A dribbles the ball and repeats the same movement.

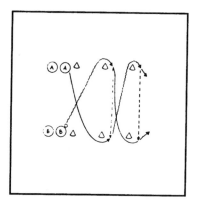

Objective: Straight-line trajectory
Difficulty: 3
No. of players: Groups of 6-8
Material: 3-4 balls and 4 cones
Description: Players A and B dribble the ball toward the two flags which form a goal mouth; they make a touch between the cones, pass on the outside and dribble up to the opposing group.

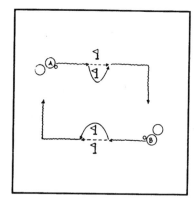

Objective: Straight-line trajectory
Difficulty: 3
No. of players: Groups of 5-6
Material: 4 balls and two cones
Description: Players A and B dribble in a straight line; when they meet, they change direction toward the right to circle the flag and move toward the opposite line.

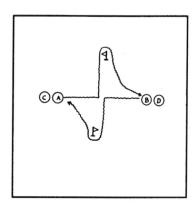

Objective: Straight-line trajectory
Difficulty: 2
No. of players: Groups of 4
Material: Two balls and a zone marked off by the team.
Description: Competition in teams. Player A dribbles up to zone C/D; when he arrives there, he deposits his ball and C dribbles his ball up to the A/B zone. The movement is repeated until players A, B, C, and D have changed their zone. The team that spends less time in the exchange is the winner.

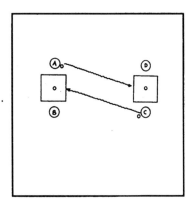

Objective: Straight-line trajectory
Difficulty: 3
No. of players: Groups of 3-4
Material: 2-3 balls per group
Description: Player A dribbles the ball up to the cone and returns to the starting point. During the round trip route the player makes a self-pass.

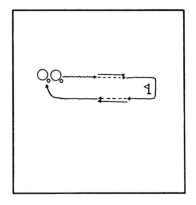

Objective: Straight-line trajectory
Difficulty: 3
No. of players: Groups of 4-5
Material: 4 balls and 4 cones per team
Description: Players A, B and C dribble up to the first cone and return to the starting point to go toward the second cone and so on. The next players start when the player ahead of them reaches the 2nd cone.

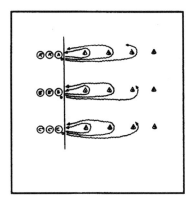

Objective: Straight-line trajectory
Difficulty: 3
No. of players: Any number
Material: One ball per player
Description: Players dribble the ball in a straight line through the field. Depending on which arm the coach raises, dribbling is done with the right or left foot.

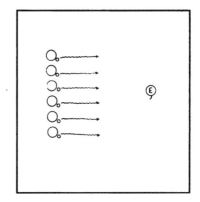

Objective: Straight-line trajectory
Difficulty: 2
No. of players: Groups of 4-5
Material: 4-5 balls, 1 cone, 1 flag
Description: Player A dribbles the ball up to the cone, leaves the ball there and runs around the flag to get the ball again and dribble it up to the starting line.

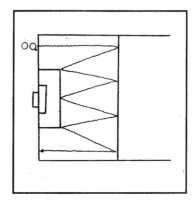

Objective: Straight-line trajectory
Difficulty: 2
No. of players: One
Material: One ball per player
Description: The players dribble the ball from line to line. End line to the midfield line, to the corner of the 18-yard box, to the midfield line, to the middle of 18-yard line, to the midfield line, to the other corner of the 18-yard box, to the midfield line and finally back to the end line.

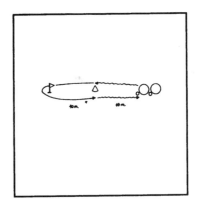

Objective: Straight-line trajectory
Difficulty: 2
No. of players: One
Material: One ball per player
Description: The players dribble the ball along all the field lines, as indicated in the diagram.

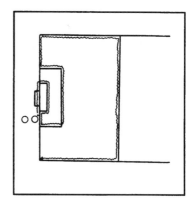

Objective: Straight-line trajectory
Difficulty: 2
No. of players: Groups of 4
Material: One ball per group
Description: Start with two players on either side of the 18-yard box on the end line. One player has a ball and dribbles around the perimeter of the penalty area and gives the ball to the next player who dribbles in the opposite direction and so on.

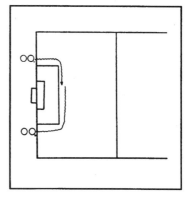

Dribbling with a curving-line trajectory

Objective: Curving-line trajectory
Difficulty: 2
No. of players: Groups of 4-5
Material: 2-3 balls and 4-5 cones per group.
Description: Player A covers the circuit, making a complete turn at each cone. The next player starts when the player in front of him reaches the 2nd cone.

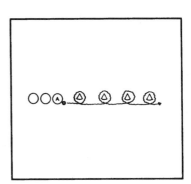

Objective: Curving-line trajectory
Difficulty: 3
No. of players: Groups of 3-4
Material: 2-3 balls and one cone per group
Description: The groups are positioned as indicated in the diagram. Players A and B go toward the cone of the opposing group on the outside of the circle; they circle it and return to their cone on the inside of the circle.

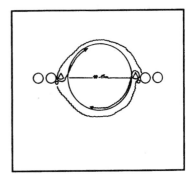

Objective: Curving-line trajectory
Difficulty: 3
No. of players: Groups of 5-6
Material: 2-3 balls and 5 flags
Description: Player A, after going around the center flag and returning to flag 1, goes toward flag 2 to go around it and again to the center flag, etc.

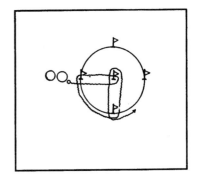

Objective: Curving-line trajectory
Difficulty: 3
No. of players: Groups of 2
Material: 2 balls and one hoop per group
Description: Players A and B each have a ball and chase each other around a hoop.

Objective: Curving-line trajectory
Difficulty: 3
No. of players: Groups of 3-4
Material: 3-4 balls and two cones per group
Description: Player A dribbles the ball from one flag to another, going around them in a figure-eight formation.

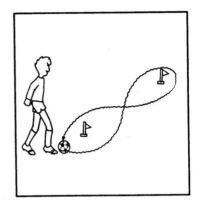

Objective: Curving-line trajectory
Difficulty: 3
No. of players: Groups of 3-4
Material: 2-3 balls and two flags per group
Description: Player A dribbles the ball from flag to flag, making a complete turn around each.

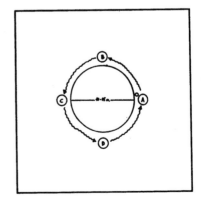

Objective: Curving-line trajectory
Difficulty: 3
No. of players: Groups of 4
Material: 4 balls per group
Description: Each player has a ball and is positioned at his own cone. At the coach's signal, they dribble clockwise or counter-clockwise trying to be the first to the next cone.

Objective: Curving-line trajectory
Difficulty: 3
No. of players: Groups of 4-5
Material: 4-5 balls per group and two cones per group
Description: The players dribble the ball around the outside of the circle until they get to the cone. Then they turn and dribble around the inside of the circle.

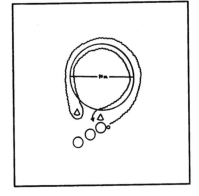

Objective: Curving-line trajectory
Difficulty: 3
No. of players: Groups of 4-5
Material: 2 balls per group
Description: Player B is positioned on the inside of a circle and tries to prevent player A from penetrating it. Player A dribbles the ball around the circle and must look for the suitable moment to enter the circle. If he ends his run without being able to enter the circle he must give way to another teammate to try.

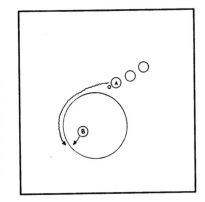

Objective: Curving-line trajectory
Difficulty: 3
No. of players: Various groups
Material: 4 balls and 4 cones per group
Description: The players are positioned as the diagram indicates. Each player must make the complete run going around each cone without another player catching him.

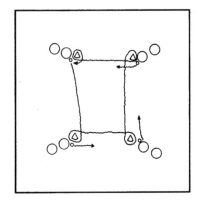

Objective: Curving-line trajectory
Difficulty: 3
No. of players: Various groups
Material: 4 balls and 6 cones per group
Description: Each group begins the exercise at the same time. They must make the entire run as indicated in the diagram. The player who finishes first earns a point for his team.

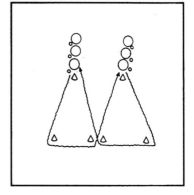

Objective: Curving-line trajectory
Difficulty: 3
No. of players: Groups of 2
Material: One ball per group
Description: Player A with the ball must try to follow the trajectory that is described by player B who runs in front of him without the ball.

Dribbling with zig-zag trajectory

Objective: Zig-zag trajectory
Difficulty: 2
No. of players: Groups of 4-5
Material: 2-3 balls and 5 cones per group
Description: Player A dribbles between the cones until arriving next to B who repeats the exercise in the opposite direction.

Objective: Zig-zag trajectory
Difficulty: 3
No. of players: Groups of 4-5
Material: 2-3 balls and 4 cones per group
Description: Players A and B dribble the ball weaving (or dodging) in and out of the cones. When they reach the last cone they make a pass to their teammates C and D who repeat the exercise.

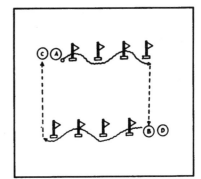

Objective: Zig-zag trajectory
Difficulty: 3
No. of players: Groups of 4-5
Material: 2-3 balls and 5 cones per group
Description: Player A dribbles the ball weaving between the cones until he reaches teammate B who repeats the exercise.

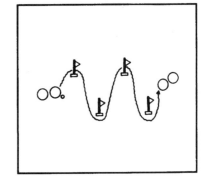

Objective: Zig-zag trajectory
Difficulty: 3
No. of players: Groups of 4-5
Material: 2-3 balls and 8-10 cones per group
Description: Player A dribbles the ball weaving through the cones, when he arrives at the last one he makes a pass to his teammate B who dribbles around the final cone and passes to the next player in line to begin the exercise again.

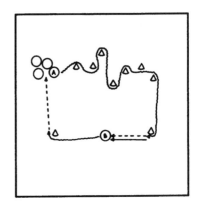

Objective: Zig-zag trajectory
Difficulty: 4
No. of players: Groups of 4-5
Material: 2-3 balls and 8-10 cones per group.
Description: Player A dribbles the ball weaving through all the cones. In the middle of his run he makes a pass to B, who returns it to him so that he continues dribbling and at the last cone he gives a pass to C who begins the exercise again.

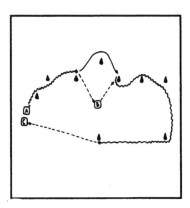

Objective: Zig-zag trajectory
Difficulty: 4
No. of players: Groups of 4-5
Material: 2-3 balls and 8-10 cones per group
Description: Player A dribbles the ball passing through the gates formed by the cones set out in an irregular way throughout the field. The players cannot skip any gate.

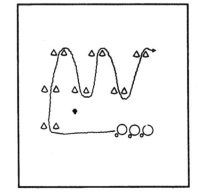

Objective: Zig-zag trajectory
Difficulty: 4
No. of players: Groups 4-5
Material: 2-3 balls and 8-10 cones per group
Description: Exercise similar to the previous one. In this case the exercise is done in pairs and the team winning the race gets the point.

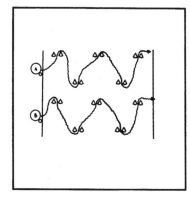

Objective: Zig-zag trajectory
Difficulty: 4
No. of players: Groups of 4-5
Material: 2-3 balls and 6-7 cones per group
Description: Each player must cover the entire area as the diagram indicates. Once finished the player must return to the starting point.

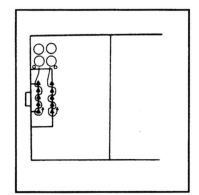

Objective: Zig-zag trajectory
Difficulty: 4
No. of players: Groups of 4-5
Material: 2-3 balls and 6-7 cones per group
Description: Each player dribbles his ball in a straight line through the field of play. The last player dribbles to the front of the line by zig-zagging through all the other players. When he reaches the front, the player who is now last in line does the same and so on.

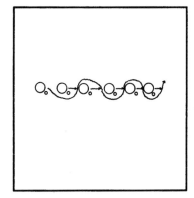

Objective: Zig-zag trajectory
Difficulty: 4
No. of players: Any number
Material: One ball per player
Description: The whole group dribbles in a straight line through the field of play and a dribbler dribbles in a crossing formation from side to side, weaving in and out (dodging) through all the players.

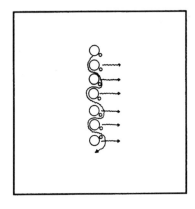

Objective: Zig-zag trajectory
Difficulty: 3
No. of players: Groups of 3
Material: 2-3 balls and 5 cones per group
Description: Players run along the lines of the penalty area. At each line they must go back to the previous line, and when they arrive at the last line, they return through a row of cones dribbling in zig-zag formation.

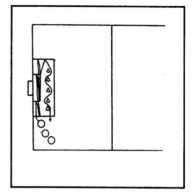

Objective: Zig-zag trajectory
Difficulty: 3
No. of players: Groups of 2
Material: One ball per group and 6 cones
Description: Players A and B crisscross among themselves passing the ball; after each cross they go around their respective cones to begin the cross again.

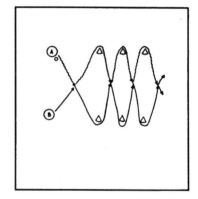

Objective: Zig-zag trajectory
Difficulty: 3
No. of players: Groups of 2
Material: One ball per group and 6 cones
Description: Players A and B, one with the ball and another without, cross each other to go toward their respective cones with a zig-zag trajectory every 2 cones.

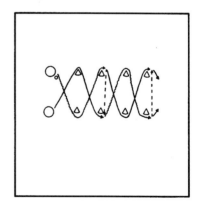

Dribbling and Passing

Objective: Dribbling + passing
Difficulty: 3
No. of players: Groups of 6-8
Material: 3-4 balls and two cones per group
Description: Player A dribbles toward midfield, dodges the cone and makes a deep pass to B who controls and dribbles toward the goalmouth. He has 2 options: 1st–Dribble to the inside cone for a straight shot. 2nd–Dribble wide for a cross or a chip shot.

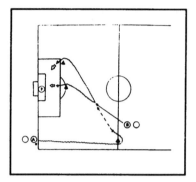

Objective: Dribbling + passing
Difficulty: 3
No. of players: Groups of 6-8
Material: 3-4 balls and one cone per group
Description: Player A dribbles from midfield; when he arrives at the cone he serves a pass to teammate B who controls, dribbles and crosses into the goalmouth for A to finish.

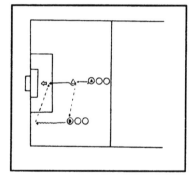

Objective: Dribbling + passing
Difficulty: 3
No. of players: Groups of 8-10
Material: 4-5 balls and two cones per group
Description: Distribution in 3 groups. The first player in one A group dribbles the ball around the cones until arriving at the goal line, where he makes a direct pass back to B who shoots. Alternate sides.

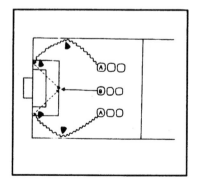

Objective: Dribbling + passing
Difficulty: 4
No. of players: Groups of 4-6
Material: 2-4 balls and two cones per group
Description: Players A and A1 throw one ball in the air and catch it (juggle) while dribbling the other ball up to the opposite cone and pass both balls to players B and B1 to control and repeat the exercise in the opposite direction.

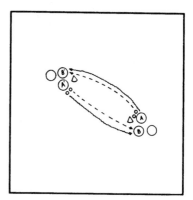

Objective: Dribbling + passing
Difficulty: 4
No. of players: Groups of 5-6
Material: 3-4 balls per group
Description: There should be 3-4 stationary players (A,B,C) standing in a row. Another player dribbles parallel to the row, making a give and go with each stationary player along the way.

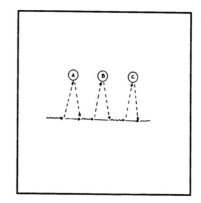

Objective: Dribbling + passing
Difficulty: 4
No. of players: Groups of 5-6
Material: 3-4 balls per group
Description: Exercise similar to the previous one with one extra condition: the dribbling and the pass are performed with both feet alternately.

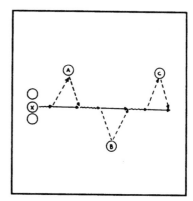

Objective: Dribbling + passing
Difficulty: 4
No. of players: Groups of 6-8
Material: 3-4 balls and two cones per group
Description: Players A and B dribble up to the cone, where they exchange balls and dribble up to the end of the run.

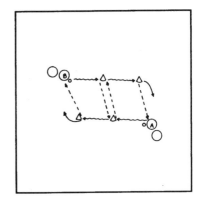

Objective: Dribbling + passing
Difficulty: 4
No. of players: Groups of 6-8
Material: Circuit of 4 cones and 4 balls per group
Description: The cones mark off a circuit with the dribble-pass concept for the development of the wall-pass. Several stationary players are required. A dribbles the ball around the circuit, making wall passes with each stationary player along the way.

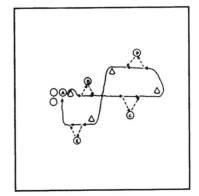

Objective: Dribbling + passing
Difficulty: 3
No. of players: Groups of 8-10
Material: 4-5 balls and 3 cones per group
Description: Player A dribbles up to the goal line and passes to the goal mouth for B to shoot. At the same time goalie C throws the ball toward A who controls and dribbles up to the starting point

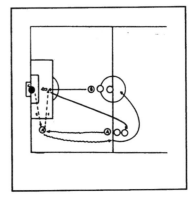

Objective: Dribbling + passing
Difficulty: 2
No. of players: Groups of 3-4
Material: One ball and two cones per group
Description: Player A dribbles the ball up to the cone, circles it and makes a pass to his teammate B. After the pass he goes to the end of the line.

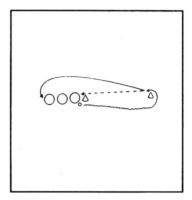

Objective: Dribbling + passing
Difficulty: 3
No. of players: Groups of 5-6
Material: 2-3 balls and a hurdle per group
Description: Player A dribbles the ball up to the cone, dodging the hurdle to the right or left. After circling the cone, he chips a pass over the hurdle toward B and goes to the end of the line.

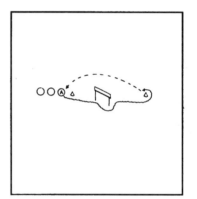

Objective: Dribbling + passing
Difficulty: 3
No. of players: Groups of 6-8
Material: One ball and one flag per group
Description: The players are in a circle. The player with the ball goes to the center of the circle, goes around the flag, makes a pass to one of his teammates and sprints to take his place. The player who receives the pass repeats the exercise and so on.

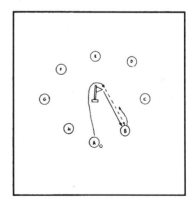

Objective: Dribbling + passing
Difficulty: 3
No. of players: Groups of 2
Material: One ball per group
Description: Player A dribbles the ball around his teammate B. When he arrives back at the starting point he sends a pass to B, who repeats the exercise.

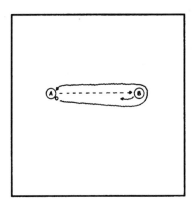

Objective: Dribbling + passing
Difficulty: 3
No. of players: Groups of 2
Material: One ball and 4 cones per group
Description: Player A dribbles the ball around the cones. When he gets to the last cone he sends a pass to his teammate B, who repeats the exercise. While B dribbles, A returns to the starting point.

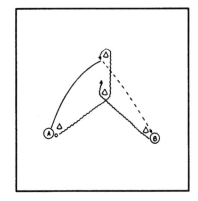

Objective: Dribbling + passing
Difficulty: 3
No. of players: Groups of 4
Material: Two balls and two cones per group
Descriptions: Dribbling and passing among players A, B, C, and D. Players A and B dribble the ball around the cone and send a diagonal pass to their respective teammates. While C and D dribble, A and B return to their starting points.

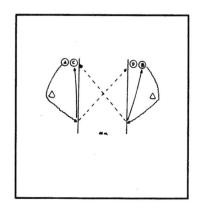

Objective: Dribbling + passing
Difficulty: 3
No. of players: Groups of 4
Material: Two balls and 6 cones per group
Description: Dribbling and passing among players A,B,C, and D. Players A and B dribble the ball toward the cone; from there each sends a deep pass for the other into space as in the diagram. They receive the pass and return to the starting point where C and D repeat the exercise.

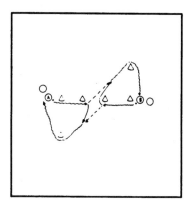

Dribbling and Shooting

Objective: Dribbling + shooting
Difficulty: 2
No. of players: Groups of 4-5
Material: 2-3 balls and two cones per group
Description: One group is positioned at each side of the penalty area. In turn, they dribble toward the center and shoot on goal.

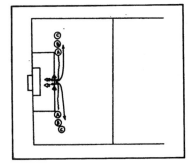

Objective: Dribbling + shooting
Difficulty: 2
No. of players: Groups of 3-4
Material: 2-3 balls and one cone per group
Description: Players dribble the ball in a straight line up to the cones and shoot on goal.

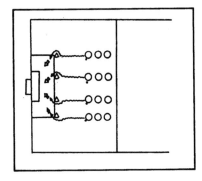

Objective: Dribbling + shooting
Difficulty: 3
No. of players: Groups of 4-5
Material: 2-3 balls and 4 cones per group
Description: One group is positioned at each side of the penalty area. The players dribble to the goal line and back to the 18-yard line before shooting on goal.

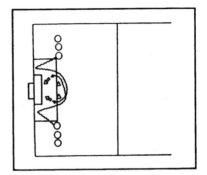

Objective: Dribbling + shooting
Difficulty: 3
No. of players: Groups of 4-5
Material: 2-3 balls per group
Description: One group is positioned at each side of the penalty area on the goal line. The players dribble along the perimeter of the area until they reach the center of the 18-yard line and shoot on goal.

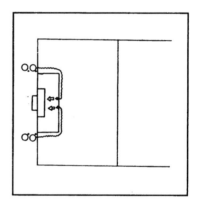

Objective: Dribbling + shooting
Difficulty: 4
No. of players: Groups of 4-5
Material: 2-3 balls per group and a cone
Description: Two groups are positioned in the midfield, one without a ball and the other with a ball. Player A dribbles towards the cone in front of the penalty area and gives the ball to B as they pass. B takes the ball, dribbles to the edge of the penalty area and shoots on goal.

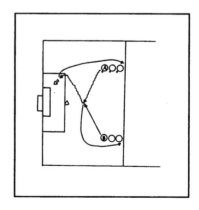

Objective: Dribbling + shooting
Difficulty: 3
No. of players: Groups of 8-10
Material: 3-4 balls per group
Description: Similar exercise to the previous one. In this exercise B intersects behind A without getting the ball. A continues with the ball and makes a pass to B who controls and shoots on goal.

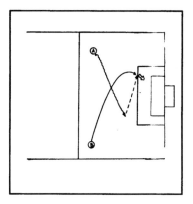

Objective: Dribbling + shooting
Difficulty: 4
No. of players: Groups of 4-5
Material: 4 balls per group
Description: The 4 cones located on the 18-yard line are the shooting areas where player A running with the ball will make a complete revolution and shoot on goal, moving quickly in search of the next ball to repeat.

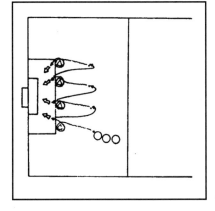

Objective: Dribbling + shooting
Difficulty: 2
No. of players: Groups of 4-5
Material: 4-5 balls and 4 cones
Description: Players A and B dribble the ball as indicated in the diagram and shoot on the goal defended by player P.

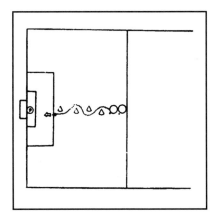

Objective: Dribbling + shooting
Difficulty: 3
No. of players: Groups of 4-5
Material: 4-5 balls and 4 cones
Description: Players A and B dribble the ball, as is indicated in the diagram, in order to finish shooting to the goalmouth defended by player P.

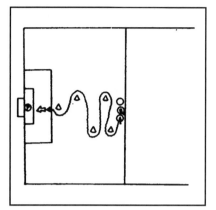

Objective: Dribbling + shooting
Difficulty: 2
No. of players: Groups of 4-5
Material: 4-5 balls and 2 cones
Description: Player A dribbles the ball in a straight line toward the goalmouth making a revolution around each cone and shoots on goal.

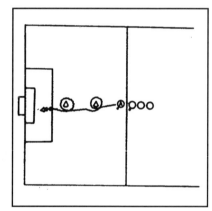

Objective: Dribbling + shooting
Difficulty: 3
No. of players: Groups of 4-5
Material: 4-5 balls and 3 cones
Description: Players A and B dribble the ball as in the diagram, circling each cone before shooting on goal.

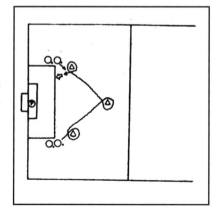

Objective: Dribbling + shooting
Difficulty: 3
No. of players: Various groups
Material: 4-5 balls and 3 cones
Description: Players A and B dribble the ball as in the diagram and shoot on the goal defended by P.

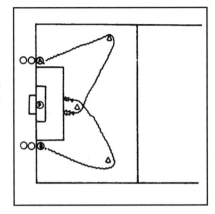

Objective: Dribbling + shooting
Difficulty: 3
No. of players: Various groups
Material: 4-5 balls
Description: Players A and B dribble the ball as in the diagram and shoot on the goal defended by P.

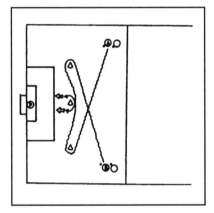

Objective: Dribbling + shooting
Difficulty: 3
No. of players: Groups of 4-5
Material: 4-5 balls and 6 cones
Description: Players A and B dribble the ball as in the diagram and shoot on the goal defended by P.

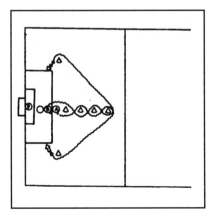

Objective: Dribbling + shooting
Difficulty: 3
No. of players: Various groups
Material: 4-5 balls and 3 cones
Description: Players A and B dribble the ball in a straight line toward the cone to shoot on the goal defended by player P. X defenders go after them to prevent the shot.

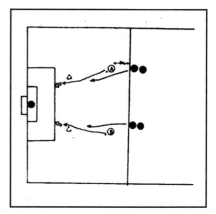

Objective: Dribbling + shooting
Difficulty: 3
No. of players: Various groups
Material: 4-5 balls and 3 cones
Description: Players A and B dribble toward the cone to shoot on the goal defended by player P, and the X players sprint to prevent the shot.

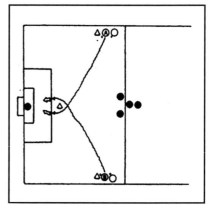

Objective: Dribbling + shooting
Difficulty: 4
No. of players: Various groups
Material: 4-5 balls and 8 cones
Description: Players A and B dribble the ball as in the diagram to shoot on the goal defended by player P. When they pass by the last cone the X defenders sprint to prevent the shot.

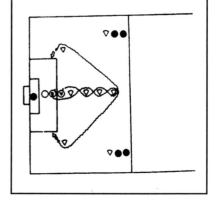

Objective: Dribbling + shooting
Difficulty: 3
No. of players: Various groups
Material: 4-5 balls and 5 cones
Description: Players A and B dribble the ball to shoot on the goal defended by player P. Players X, when A and B pass by the cone, go after the ball to prevent the shot.

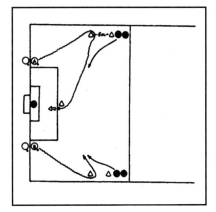

Objective: Dribbling + shooting
Difficulty: 4
No. of players: Various groups
Material: 4-5 balls and 5 cones
Description: Players A and B dribble the ball as in the diagram and shoot on the goal defended by player P. The X players go after the ball when A and B go around the cone and move toward the goal.

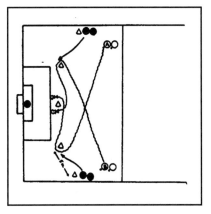

Objective: Dribbling + shooting
Difficulty: 3
No. of players: Groups of 2
Material: One ball and 2 cones per group
Description: Player A dribbles the ball up to midfield; from there he makes a deep pass to his teammate B, who has made a breaking move; B has the option of shooting to the first goalpost or making a dribble on the diagonal to look for the better shot.

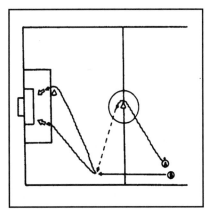

Dribbling with opponents present

Objective: Dribbling with opponents present
Difficulty: 3
No. of players: Groups of 2
Material: One ball per group
Description: Player B chases his teammate A and tries to touch him. Then they change roles. The player who has gone around the circle more times before being touched wins.

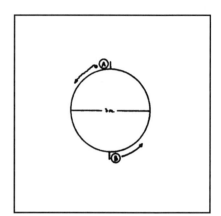

Objective: Dribbling with opponents present
Difficulty: 3
No. of players: Groups of 3
Material: One ball and 4 cones per group
Description: Player C tries to dribble up to cone X before being touched by his teammates A and B who start the chase at the same time.

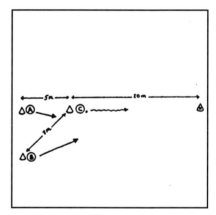

Objective: Dribbling with opponents present
Difficulty: 3
No. of players: Various groups
Material: One ball and 4 cones per group
Description: Player A tries to dribble around the entire circuit without being caught by the players who are stationed at the cones. These players begin the chase as soon as A passes their cone.

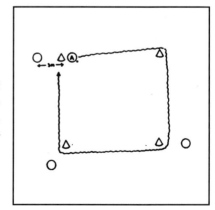

Objective: Dribbling with opponents present
Difficulty: 3
No. of players: Groups of 3
Material: One ball and 4 cones per group
Description: Player A tries to dribble up to cone X. Players B and C, who come out at the same time, try to touch him before he gets to the cone.

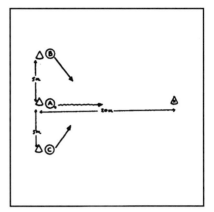

Objective: Dribbling with opponents present
Difficulty: 3
No. of players: Groups of 3
Material: One ball and 4 cones per group
Description: Player C makes a pass to his teammate B who begins a fast dribble toward cone X, trying to avoid being touched by player A: Player A leaves when the pass is made.

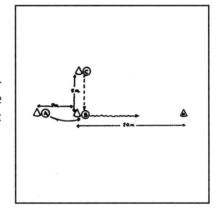

Objective: Dribbling with opponents present
Difficulty: 3
No. of players: Groups of 3
Material: One ball and 4 cones per group
Description: Player A tries to touch the player who dribbles the ball toward cone X. Before beginning the dribble, players B and C exchange 3-4 passes among themselves to try to trick player A, who can't move until one of them begins the dribble.

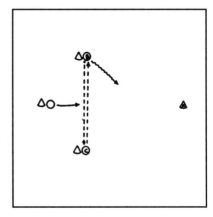

Objective: Dribbling with opponents present
Difficulty: 3
No. of players: Groups of 3
Material: One ball per group
Description: Two players with a ball dribble through the field of play pursued by a third without a ball who tries to steal it from them.

Objective: Dribbling with opponents present
Difficulty: 3
No. of players: Groups of 2
Material: One ball and 3 cones per group
Description: Player B passes the ball into the run of A who is headed toward cone X. Player B, after the pass, sprints to prevent A from reaching the cone.

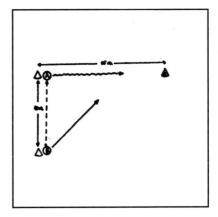

Objective: Dribbling with opponents present
Difficulty: 3
No. of players: Groups of 2
Material: One ball per group
Description: Two players go hand in hand. One of them dribbles the ball and the other tries to steal it from him.

Objective: Dribbling with opponents present
Difficulty: 3
No. of players: Various groups
Material: 4-5 balls and 4-5 cones
Description: Player A, with a ball and starting in a crouching position, jumps up and dribbles toward the cone. Player B tries to catch up to him starting from a stretched out prone position. The players exchange roles and the one who manages to overtake his teammate more times wins.

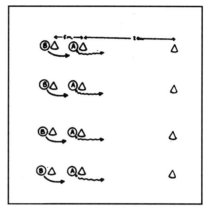

Objective: Dribbling with opponents present
Difficulty: 3
No. of players: Groups of 8-10
Material: One ball per player and one hoop per group
Description: Two groups of 4-5 players. Each player has a ball; on the coach's signal, the players dribble and deposit their balls inside the hoop. The last one to leave a ball is eliminated. The ball at no time can be touched with the hands.

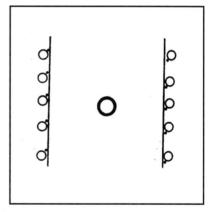

Application plays

Objective: Application plays
Difficulty: 3
No. of players: Groups of 8-10
Material: 4-5 balls per group
Description: Players, divided in pairs, are positioned at the cardinal points of a circle. At the signal, one player from each pair dribbles rapidly around the perimeter of the circle, trying to maintain the distance between himself and the dribblers in front and behind.

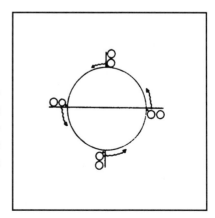

Objective: Application plays
Difficulty: 3
No. of players: Groups of 8-10
Material: 4-5 balls per group
Description: With the same set-up as the previous exercise, at the signal the player with the ball dribbles rapidly to reach the team who is running up front and at the same time avoids being overcome by the team coming from behind. However, if the coach gives another signal all the dribblers must turn and dribble in the opposite direction.

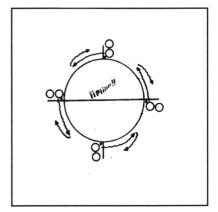

Objective: Application plays
Difficulty: 2
No. of players: Groups of 12-14
Material: 4 balls per group
Description: The players are divided into 3-4 teams. Each team is positioned in a line at equal distances apart and runs a relay with the first player starting at the signal and the other players starting as their dribbling teammate reaches them.

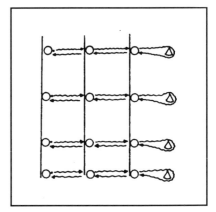

Objective: Application plays
Difficulty: 2
No. of players: Groups of 10-15
Material: One ball per player
Description: Each player dribbles his ball throughout the field of play avoiding any contact with other players. They dribble slowly at first and increase the dribbling rhythm as they gain confidence.

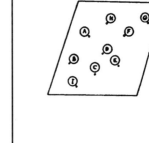

Objective: Application plays
Difficulty: 3
No. of players: Groups of 10-15
Material: One ball per pair
Description: The players are divided into two equal-numbered teams. On one team each player has a ball, while the other team starts without any balls. The team without the ball tries to steal all the balls from the opposing team. The winning team is the one who manages to steal all the balls in the shortest time.

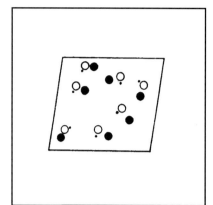

Objective: Application plays
Difficulty: 2
No. of players: Groups of 10-15
Material: One ball per player
Description: All the players have a ball except for 2 or 3. The players without a ball try to steal all the balls from their teammates. The players who lose their ball are eliminated.

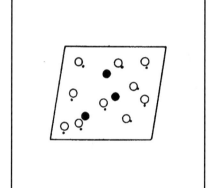

Objective: Application plays
Difficulty: 3
No. of players: Groups of 10-15
Material: One ball per player and 4 marked zones.
Description: All the players with a ball dribble through the field without entering the marked zones. At the coach's signal they enter the zones. The last player into the zone is eliminated.

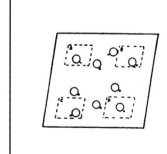

Objective: Application plays
Difficulty: 4
No. of players: Groups of 10-15
Material: One ball per player
Description: The players are on equal-numbered teams. Each team must try to dispossess the players on the opposite team without losing their own balls.

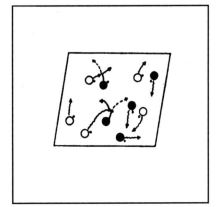

Objective: Application plays
Difficulty: 3
No. of players: Groups of 5
Material: 5 balls and 4 cones
Description: There is a player at each cone and one in the center. At the signal all the players must move from one cone to another. If the center player gets to a cone before another player, that player moves to the center.

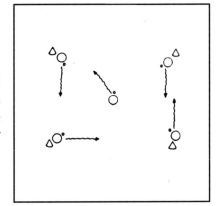

Objective: Application plays
Difficulty: 4
No. of players: Groups of 10-15
Material: 6-8 balls per group
Description: Two equal-numbered teams: Each team has 4 balls which they must try to keep.

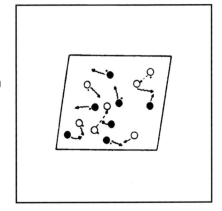

Objective: Application plays
Difficulty: 3
No. of players: Various groups
Material: One ball per player and 5 cones
Description: All the players dribble freely though the field of play and at the coach's signal must go toward the designated cone. The last to arrive is eliminated.

Objective: Application plays
Difficulty: 3
No. of players: Various groups
Material: 4-5 balls and two hoops per group
Description: 6 v 6 to try to take the maximum number of balls to their respective hoops; the ball in no way can be touched with the hands.

Objective: Application plays
Difficulty: 3
No. of players: Various groups
Material: 4-5 balls and 8 cones per group
Description: Four teams of 3 players each, each with a ball, dribble collectively around the perimeter marked with cones. Every 3 laps, the coach determines which team is farthest behind and eliminates one player from that team. If a team or some member manages to trap the previous group, 2 players are eliminated.

CHAPTER 3
PASSES
Short passes
Individual exercises

Objective: Short passes (Individual ex.)
Difficulty: 2
No. of players: One
Material: One ball per player
Description: The player dribbles through the field of play making self passes; after reaching the ball he changes direction making another self pass.

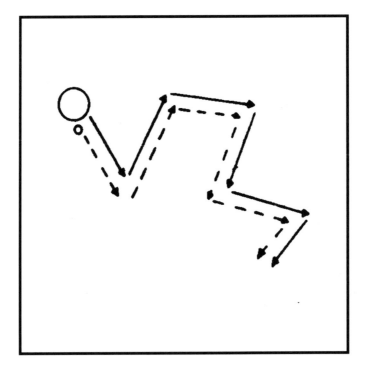

Objective: Short passes (Individual ex.)
Difficulty: 3
No. of players: One
Material: One ball per player
Description: The player dribbles through the field of play making self passes, trying to draw a square on the ground with the path he describes with the ball.

Objective: Short passes (Individual ex.)
Difficulty: 3
No. of players: One
Material: One ball per player
Description: The player dribbles through the field of play making self passes in a zig-zag trajectory.

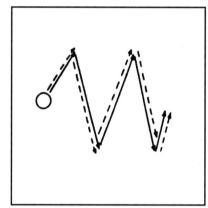

Objective: Short passes (Individual ex.)
Difficulty: 4
No. of players: One
Material: One ball per player
Description: One player is positioned on a surface limited by two lines.
From one line he passes the ball toward the other line and sprints to receive it before it reaches the line. He continues from one line to the other for a set period of time or number of passes.

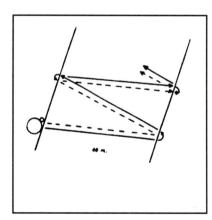

Exercises with groups of 2

Objective: Short passes (between 2 players)
Difficulty: 2
No. of players: Groups of 2
Material: One ball per player
Description: Players A and B pass each other the ball at first touch with different trajectories; ex. A sends with a lobbed trajectory and B returns it with a low-to-the-ground skimming trajectory.

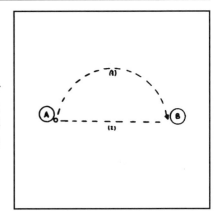

Objective: Short passes (between 2 players)
Difficulty: 2
No. of players: Groups of 2
Material: One ball and one hurdle per group
Description: Passes between players A and B. While A passes the ball over the obstacle, player B returns it under the hurdle.

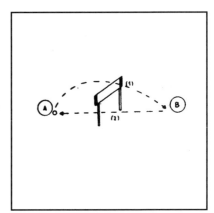

Objective: Short passes (between 2 players)
Difficulty: 3
No. of players: Groups of 2
Material: One ball and one hurdle per group
Description: Passes with a curving-line trajectory between players A and B. Each player makes his pass to his teammate around the hurdle.

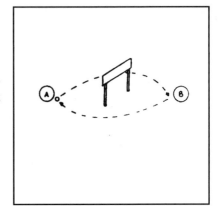

Objective: Short passes (between 2 players)
Difficulty: 3
No. of players: Groups of 4
Material: One ball per group
Description: Players A and B make passes between themselves trying to avoid the opposition (blockage) of C and D, who at each pass increase their separation.

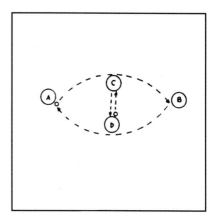

Objective: Short passes (between 2 players)
Difficulty: 3
No. of players: Groups of 2
Material: One ball and one hurdle per group
Description: Passes between A and B. Player A sends the ball to his teammate using all the possible trajectories (above, below and on the sides of the hurdle.) Player B answers the passes of A with the same trajectory.

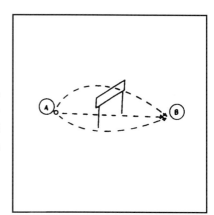

Objective: Short passes (between 2 players)
Difficulty: 2
No. of players: Groups of 2
Material: One ball per group
Description: Players move in a parallel formation through the field of play passing the ball back and forth. Variants: pass with different trajectories.

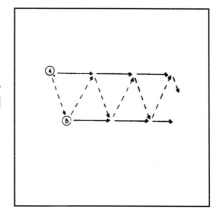

Objective: Short passes (between 2 players)
Difficulty: 2
No. of players: Groups of 2
Material: One ball per group
Description: Players move in a parallel formation through the field of play, passing the ball back and forth. Before making the pass to his teammate, each player dribbles the ball for two or three strides.

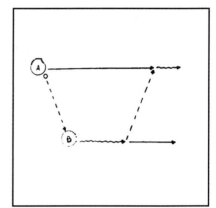

Objective: Short passes (between 2 players)
Difficulty: 3
No. of players: Groups of 2
Material: One ball per group
Description: Players A and B pass the ball among themselves. Starting at cone 1, they must retreat to cone 2 and return again to cone 1 to receive a new pass.

Objective: Short passes (between 2 players)
Difficulty: 2
No. of players: Groups of 2
Material: One ball per group
Description: The player sends a pass that passes over the head of B; B runs to receive it to send a similar pass to A, who has passed by him after having made the pass.

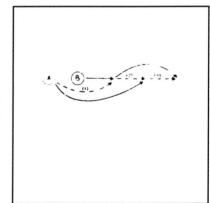

Objective: Short passes (between 2 players)
Difficulty: 3
No. of players: Groups of 2
Material: One ball and 5 cones per group
Description: Players A and B are positioned at either side of the cones and move in a parallel formation through the field of play: they must pass the ball to each other trying to make it pass between the cones.

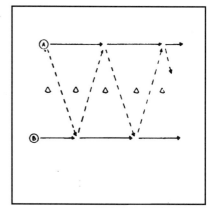

Objective: Short passes (between 2 players)
Difficulty: 4
No. of players: Groups of 2
Material: Two balls per group
Description: Players A and B pass their ball at the same time that they receive their team-mate's ball. If in the process of these exchanges the balls collide and deviate from their original trajectory each player must go get the ball from the opponent and from there begin the exercise again.

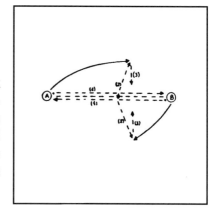

Objective: Short passes (between 2 players)
Difficulty: 3
No. of players: Groups of 2
Material: One ball per group
Description: Player A has possession of the ball. When A sends the ball forward, B must run to retrieve it and make a new pass that will be run down by A, etc.

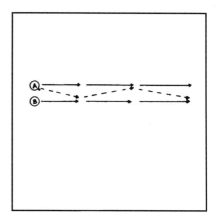

Objective: Short passes (between 2 players)
Difficulty: 3
No. of players: Groups of 2
Material: One ball per group
Description: Player A dribbles the ball and gives a forward pass so that B, who runs parallel to him, retrieves. At the same time A goes to occupy teammate B's place. B repeats the exercise with a forward pass for A.

Objective: Short passes (between 2 players)
Difficulty: 3
No. of players: Groups of 2
Material: Two balls per group
Description: A and B each have a ball and dribble in a parallel formation. Every few feet they simultaneously make a pass into the path of their teammate, control the pass and continue dribbling.

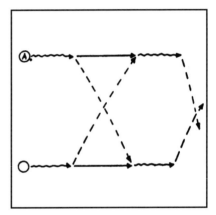

Objective: Short pass (between 2 players)
Difficulty: 3
No. of players: Groups of 2
Material: Two balls per group
Description: A and B each have a ball and dribble in a parallel formation. Every few feet they simultaneously pass the ball forward and run to retrieve the pass made by their teammate. After controlling the ball, they make another pass and so on.

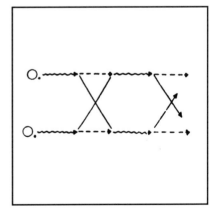

Objective: Short passes (between 2 players)
Difficulty: 3
No. of players: Groups of 2
Material: One ball per group
Description: Player A with a ball and B without a ball criss-cross. After passing by each other, A turns and passes the ball into the path of B, who controls it and turns to repeat the move, criss-crossing with A, turning and passing into the path of A and so on.

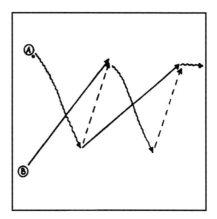

Objective: Short passes (between 2 players)
Difficulty: 3
No. of players: Groups of 2
Material: Two balls per group
Description: Players A and B each have a ball and dribble in a parallel formation. At the same time, they pass the ball forward and run to control their teammate's ball. They then make a lateral (square) pass, control and continue the exercise.

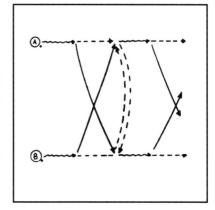

Objective: Short passes (between 2 players)
Difficulty: 3
No. of players: Groups of 2
Material: Two balls per group
Description: Players A and B dribble their ball and by means of a self-pass they exchange their positions (they follow their own pass).

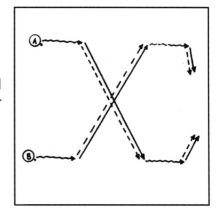

Objective: Short passes (between 2 players)
Difficulty: 3
No. of players: Groups of 2
Material: Two balls per group
Description: Players A and B dribble their ball and exchange their positions with a criss-cross, give a forward pass and criss-cross again (this time without the ball) to retrieve their teammate's pass and they repeat.

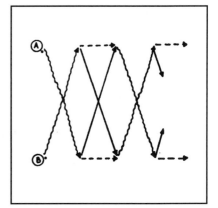

Objective: Short passes (between 2 players)
Difficulty: 3
No. of players: Groups of 2
Material: Two balls per group
Description: Players A and B dribble their ball and exchange their positions with a criss-cross, turn and give a diagonal pass for their teammate, run to retrieve the pass and they repeat the pattern.

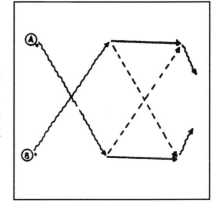

Objective: Short passes (between 2 players)
Difficulty: 2
No. of players: Groups of 2
Material: One ball per group
Description: Player A with a ball has player B at his back; when A makes a pass forward, B runs by him to control it and gives a pass forward for A to retrieve and so on.

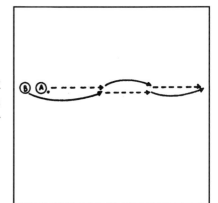

Objective: Long passes (between 2 players)
Difficulty: 3
No. of players: Groups of 2
Material: One ball per group
Description: Frontal and side passes between A and B. A makes a frontal pass so that B, after breaking away, controls the ball and makes a lateral pass to A who after breaking away will control to make a frontal pass again to B, etc.

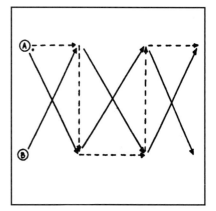

Objective: Long passes (between 2 players)
Difficulty: 3
No. of players: Groups of 2
Material: One ball per group
Description: Passes between players A and B; player A makes a diagonal pass forward and player B makes a diagonal pass backward.

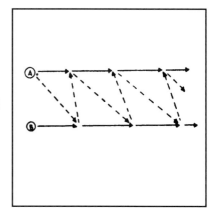

Objective: Long passes (between 2 players)
Difficulty: 3
No. of players: Groups of 2
Material: One ball per group
Description: Passes between players A and B; player A makes a lateral pass and player B makes a diagonal pass forward.

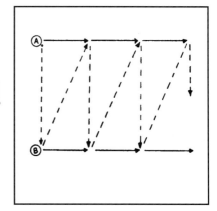

Exercises with groups of 3

Objective: Short passes (among 3 players)
Difficulty: 2
No. of players: Groups of 3
Material: One ball per group
Description: Players A, B and C located in a triangular formation pass the ball among themselves. At each signal given by the coach the direction of the passes changes.

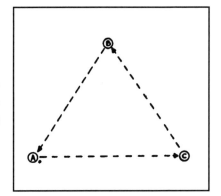

Objective: Short passes (among 3 players)
Difficulty: 2
No. of players: Groups of 3
Material: Two balls per group
Description: Player A is located between players C and D; A returns the passes that his teammates send to him alternately.

Objective: Short passes (among 3 players)
Difficulty: 3
No. of players: Groups of 3
Material: Two balls and two cones per group
Description: The player located between the two cones returns the passes that his teammates A and B send to him alternately. After returning A's pass, C runs toward the other cone to receive B's pass, etc.

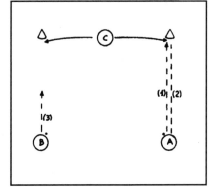

Objective: Short passes (among 3 players)
Difficulty: 3
No. of players: Groups of 3
Material: Two balls and a hurdle per group
Description: Player A, after returning a pass sent by C, jumps over the hurdle to be ready to receive teammate B's pass. (The number of repetitions is modified according to the age of the players.)

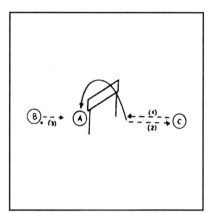

Objective: Short passes (among 3 players)
Difficulty: 2
No. of players: Groups of 3
Material: One ball per group
Description: Player A makes a self-pass; he is obligated to get the ball before arriving at teammate B's position; from there he sends the ball to B who performs the same action as A to be able to hand it over to C.

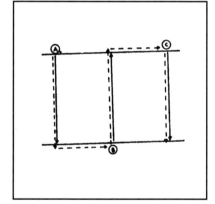

Objective: Short passes (among 3 players)
Difficulty: 3
No. of players: Groups of 3
Material: One ball per group
Description: Player A sends the ball to his teammate B who controls and prepares a frontal pass for A who has followed his pass and run around B. When A gets the ball he repeats the same action with teammate C. At each turn tasks are varied among A, B and C.

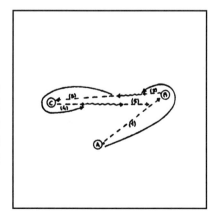

Objective: Short passes (among 3 players)
Difficulty: 3
No. of players: Groups of 3
Material: One ball per group
Description: Player B sends a frontal pass; C runs to control it; dribbles and makes another frontal pass for A who runs to get it, etc. After each pass the center player goes toward the side that has been abandoned to get the ball.

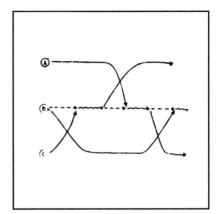

Objective: Short passes (among 3 players)
Difficulty: 3
No. of players: Groups of 3
Material: One ball per group
Description: Players A, B and C run in a parallel formation through the field of play. The ball must go to all the players, but with the provision that it passes through the center player.

Objective: Short passes (among 3 players)
Difficulty: 3
No. of players: Groups of 3
Material: One ball and 4 cones per group
Description: Player A sends a pass to B who with the first touch sends it toward teammate C. At the same time, player A runs to occupy the free space to receive the pass from C.

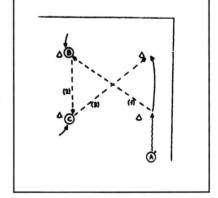

Objective: Short passes (among 3 players)
Difficulty: 3
No. of players: Groups of 3
Material: One ball and 3 cones per group
Description: Player A sends a pass to teammate B who with the first touch sends a pass to C. After making the passes, players A and B break away rapidly toward the free spaces located in front of the opposing goalmouth.

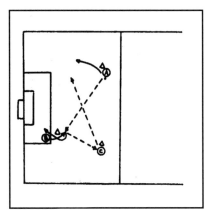

Objective: Short passes (among 3 players)
Difficulty: 3
No. of players: Groups of 3
Material: One ball per group
Description: Players A, B and C run in parallel formation through the field of play making in-depth passes and supporting from behind. Player A sends a deep pass toward B who returns the pass first time and continues his run. A does the same with C and so on.

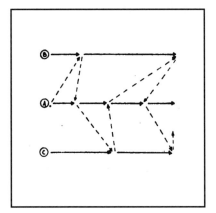

Objective: Short passes (among 3 players)
Difficulty: 3
No. of players: Groups of 3
Material: One ball and 6 cones per group
Description: Player A passes the ball to B who passes to C; C passes to A to complete the tri-angle. Each player must go around each of the two cones before receiving the next pass.

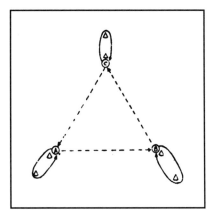

Objective: Short passes (among 3 players)
Difficulty: 3
No. of players: Groups of 3
Material: One ball and two cones per group
Description: Player A makes a pass to B and runs to occupy his place. B passes it to C and also runs to occupy his place; this exercise is repeated successfully.

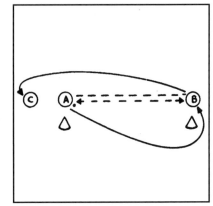

Objective: Short passes (among 3 players)
Difficulty: 3
No. of players: Groups of 3
Material: One ball per group
Description: Passes between players A and B; player A makes a pass to B who returns it to him. Player C tries to intercept the passes.

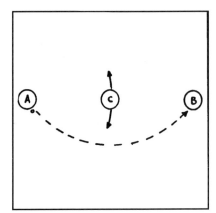

Objective: Short passes (among 3 players)
Difficulty: 3
No. of players: Groups of 3
Material: One ball per group
Description: Passes among players A, B and C. Player A makes a pass to B and goes to occupy his place. B makes a self-pass over A to control and pass to C who makes the same self-pass over B, etc.

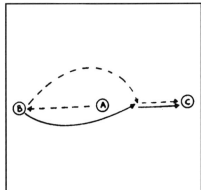

Objective: Short passes (among 3 players)
Difficulty: 3
No. of players: Groups of 3
Material: One ball and one bench per group
Description: Passes among players A,B and C:
Players A and B, after interchanging two passes
with the bench (in place), send a pass, over the
bench, toward C.

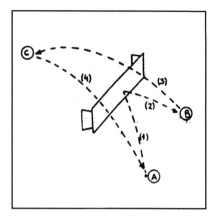

Exercises with groups of 4

Objective: Short passes (among 4 players)
Difficulty: 3
No. of players: Groups of 4
Material: One ball per group
Description: Player A receives passes from B
and C alternately, and must avoid player D
who tries to intercept the passes directed to
player A.

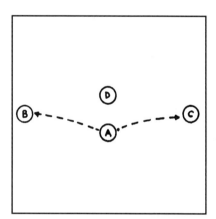

Objective: Short passes (among 4 players)
Difficulty: 2
No. of players: Groups of 4
Material: One ball per group
Description: In a small area, players A, B, C
and D pass the ball among themselves, trying
to play first touch. Vary the exercise by changing the contact surface (head, instep, thigh,
etc.).

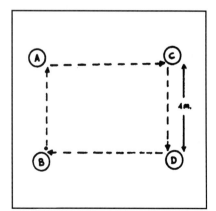

Objective: Short passes (among 4 players)
Difficulty: 3
No. of players: Groups of 4
Material: Two balls and 4 cones per group
Description: Players A, B C and D are located in a quadrangular formation. Only A and B possess a ball which they pass to their teammates C and D who after returning the pass must exchange their positions.

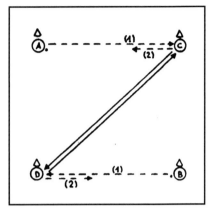

Objective: Short passes (among 4 players)
Difficulty: 3
No. of players: Groups of 4
Material: One ball and 4 cones per group
Description: Players A, B, C and D are located in a quadrangular formation. Passes are made on the diagonal and each player must exchange his position after making the pass.

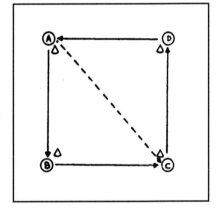

Objective: Short passes (among 4 players)
Difficulty: 3
No. of players: Groups of 4
Material: One ball per group
Description: Players A and D are located at the ends of the penalty area and their teammates B and C are in the center. Player A sends a pass to C who touches it in a backward direction over B who after controlling will send it to D. Once the ball has arrived to D the exercise begins again.

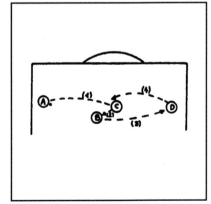

Objective: Short passes (among 4 players)
Difficulty: 4
No. of players: Groups of 4
Material: Two balls and 4 cones per group
Description: The graph indicates the players' locations. Players A and B go after and return the pass sent by their teammates C and D; Afterwards they run toward their respective cones to receive the next pass and return it.

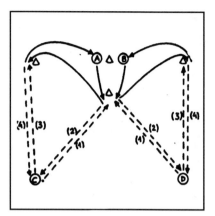

Objective: Short passes (among 4 players)
Difficulty: 4
No. of players: Groups of 4
Material: One ball per group
Description: Players A,B,C and D are located where the graph indicates and move to receive diagonal and supporting passes. Player A passes to C who in a frontal position touches in a backward direction toward his teammate B; B makes a diagonal pass to D who repeats the same action with A, etc.

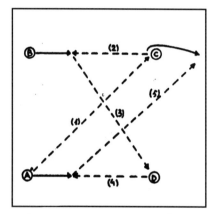

Objective: Short passes (among 4 players)
Difficulty: 4
No. of players: Groups of 4
Material: Two balls and 4 cones
Description: The graph indicates the players' positions. Player A sends a pass to B who controls, turns and passes to C who has just performed a similar action with D. Players B and D after the pass go to the X cones, where they receive a new pass that they will return to the same passer; then they will return to the Y cones, etc.

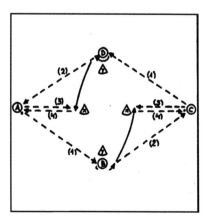

Objective: Short passes (among 4 players)
Difficulty: 3
No. of players: Groups of 4
Material: One ball per group
Description: Players are located in a quadrangular formation. The ball goes from A to B to C to D, while players A-B and C-D exchange their positions.

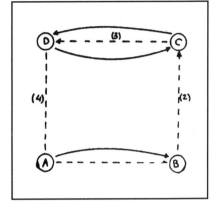

Objective: Short passes (among 4 players)
Difficulty: 3
No. of players: Groups of 4
Material: One ball per group
Description: Players are located in a quadrangular formation. The ball goes from A to B, to C and to D. After each pass each player follows the ball occupying the space adjacent to his own. When the ball gets to D he dribbles it until he reaches A's place.

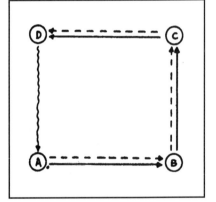

Objective: Short passes (among 4 players)
Difficulty: 3
No. of players: Groups of 4
Material: One ball per group
Description: Player A sends the ball to B who returns it to A and A gives a deep pass to C or D.

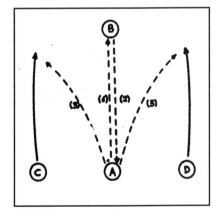

Objective: Short passes (among 4 players)
Difficulty: 3
No. of players: Groups of 4
Material: One ball per group
Description: Passes among players A,B,C,D. In a triangular formation, as indicated in the diagram, A makes a pass to B who passes to C who passes back to A who passes to D to repeat in the opposite direction.

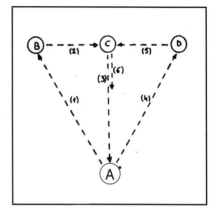

Objective: Short passes (among 4 players)
Difficulty: 3
No. of players: Groups of 4
Material: One ball per group
Description: The diagram indicates the players' positions. Players on the outer edge pass the ball among themselves but with the condition that they must first pass to A who returns the pass.

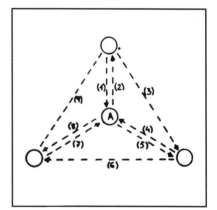

Objective: Short passes (among 4 players)
Difficulty: 3
No. of players: Groups of 4
Material: One ball per group
Description: Player A passes the ball to C and B passes to D. C and D return the pass and make a half turn to receive a new pass, this time from the player located on the opposite side.

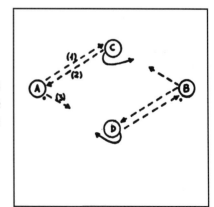

Objective: Short passes (among 4 players)
Difficulty: 3
No. of players: Groups of 4
Material: One ball and one bench per group
Description: Players exchange passes against a bench and switch positions.

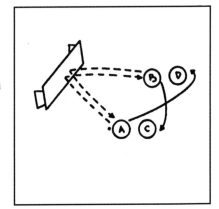

Objective: Short passes (among 4 players)
Difficulty: 3
No. of players: Groups of 4
Material: One ball and 8-12 cones per group
Description: The 4 players pass the ball among themselves without hitting any cones.

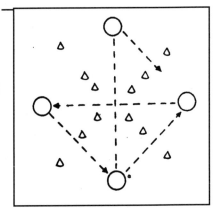

Objective: Short passes (among 4 players)
Difficulty: 3
No. of players: Groups of 4
Material: One ball per group
Description: The 4 players move in a parallel pattern though the field of play while making repeated passes from one line to the next.

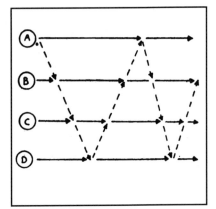

Objective: Short passes (among 4 players)
Difficulty: 3
No. of players: Groups of 4
Material: One ball an d 4 cones
Description: Players A, B and C exchange passes among themselves without leaving the zone marked by the cones. Defender X tries to intercept these passes.

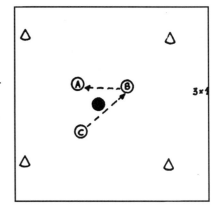

Exercises with various groups

Objective: Short passes (various groups)
Difficulty: 2
No. of players: Various groups
Material: One ball per group
Description: The players exchange passes from one side to another. After each pass the passer moves to the back of his own line.

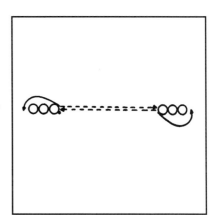

Objective: Short passes (various groups)
Difficulty: 2
No. of players: Various groups
Material: One ball per group
Description: Players exchange passes from one side to another. After each pass the passer goes to the back of the opposite line.

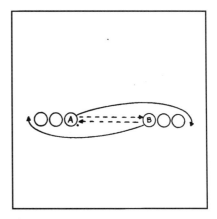

Objective: Short passes (various groups)
Difficulty: 2
No. of players: Various groups
Material: One ball per group
Description: Players A and B act as stationary players, the rest of the players send passes alternately to them, going to the back of the line once they have made 2 passes.

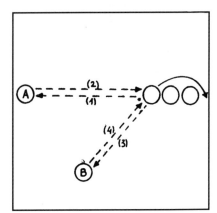

Objective: Short passes (various groups)
Difficulty: 3
No. of players: Various groups
Material: One ball per group
Description: Players A and B act as stationary players; the rest of the players send passes alternately to them. Players follow their own pass each time.

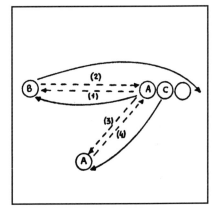

Objective: Short passes (various groups)
Difficulty: 2
No. of players: Various groups
Material: One ball and two cones per group
Description: Players from both groups exchange passes with each pass going between the cones; each player after having made the pass goes to the end of his own group.

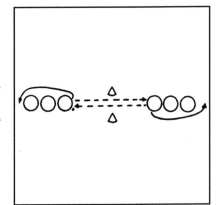

Objective: Short passes (various groups)
Difficulty: 2
No. of players: Various groups
Material: One ball and two cones per group
Description: Players from both groups exchange passes with each pass going between the cones. Each player after having made the pass goes to the end of the opposite group.

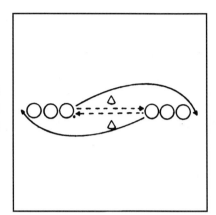

Objective: Short passes (various groups)
Difficulty: 2
No. of players: Various groups
Material: One ball and one bench per group
Description: The players of both groups exchange passes with each pass going over the bench. Each player after having made the pass goes to the end of his own group.

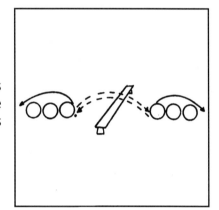

Objective: Short passes (various groups)
Difficulty: 2
No. of players: Various groups
Material: One ball and one bench per group
Description: Players from both groups exchange passes with each pass going over the bench. Each player after having made the pass goes to the end of the opposite group.

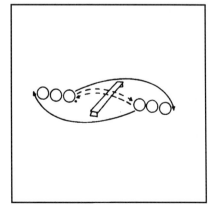

Objective: Short passes (numerous groups)
Difficulty: 3
No. of players: Various groups
Material: Two balls per group
Description: The 4 teams are placed in a quadrangular formation. The two players with a ball make a forward pass and move to the back of their own line.

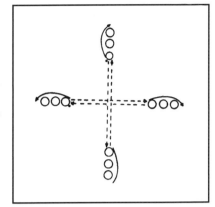

Objective: Short passes (numerous groups)
Difficulty: 3
No. of players: Various groups
Material: Two balls per group
Description: The 4 teams are placed in a quadrangular formation. The two players with a ball make a forward pass and move to the end of the line on their right.

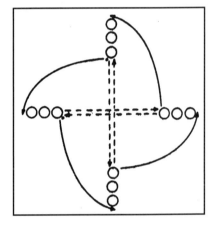

Objective: Short passes (various groups)
Difficulty: 3
No. of players: Various groups
Material: One ball per group
Description: Players are positioned in a circle with one in the center as a stationary player. The stationary player passes the ball to the outside (exterior) players in order until finishing the whole revolution.

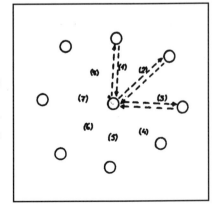

Objective: Short passes (various groups)
Difficulty: 3
No. of players: Various groups
Material: One ball per group
Description: Players are positioned in a circle with one in the center as a stationary player. The stationary player passes the ball to the outside (exterior) players in no particular order until he has passed to every player.

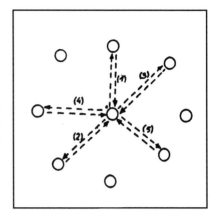

Objective: Short passes (various groups)
Difficulty: 3
No. of players: Various groups
Material: One ball per group
Description: Player A sends the ball to B who returns the ball to him first time; then A sends to C who has opened toward one side of the group and C returns the pass; successively A passes to all the members of the group who return the ball first time.

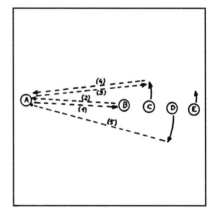

Objective: Short passes (various groups)
Difficulty: 4
No. of players: Various groups
Material: One ball per group
Description: The players are located in a circle. A passes to B who passes to C outside of the circle; C sends it to the center where A controls and returns it to him to pass to D, etc.

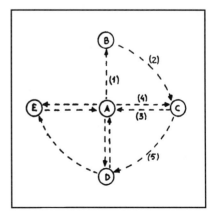

Objective: Short passes (various groups)
Difficulty: 4
No. of players: Various groups
Material: 4-5 balls per group
Description: Player A passes the ball to B who moves to meet the ball, controls and goes toward the opposing group while A changes groups.

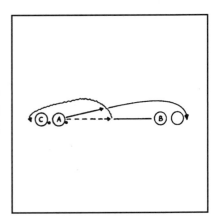

Objective: Short passes (various groups)
Difficulty: 4
No. of players: Numerous group
Material: 4-5 balls per group
Description: Player A passes the ball to B, who returns it to him, so that A controls and dribbles up to the opposing group, giving the ball to C as he goes by.

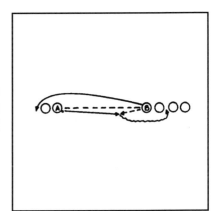

Objective: Short passes (various groups)
Difficulty: 4
No. of players: Various groups
Material: One ball per group
Description: The players are positioned at both sides of the cones and must pass the ball back and forth between the cones.

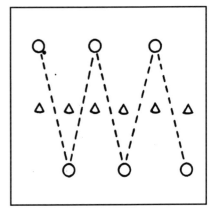

Objective: Short passes (various groups)
Difficulty: 4
No. of players: Various groups
Material: Two balls per group
Description: Players are positioned at either side of the cones and must pass 2 balls back and forth between the cones.

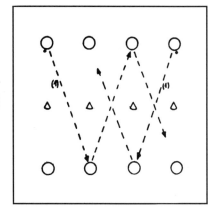

Objective: Short passes (various groups)
Difficulty: 3
No. of players: Various groups
Material: One ball per group
Description: The players are positioned in a circle with a stationary player in the center. The exterior (outside) players, after making a pass to the stationary player in the center, move to occupy their place while the stationary player goes to the place vacated by the passer.

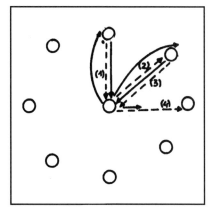

Objective: Short passes (various groups)
Difficulty: 3
No. of players: Various groups
Material: Two balls per group
Description: The same mechanics as the previous exercise with the difference that there are two balls and two stationary players.

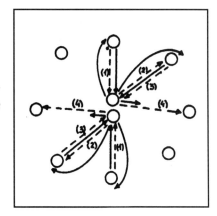

Objective: Short passes (various groups)
Difficulty: 3
No. of players: Various groups
Material: One ball per group
Description: The players are positioned in a circle and try to pass the ball in spite of the opposition of teammate A who tries to block the exterior player's passes.

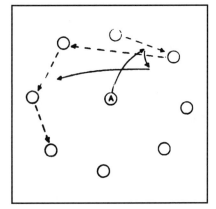

Objective: Short passes (various groups)
Difficulty: 3
No. of players: Various groups
Material: One ball per group
Description: Player A passes the ball to B; B returns it to him with a lead pass so that A receives on the run and dribbles toward the cone, where he passes to C and returns to the starting point. C passes to B to repeat the exercise.

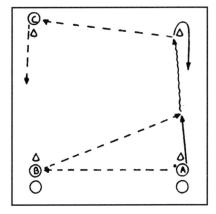

Objective: Short passes (various groups)
Difficulty: 3
No. of players: Various groups
Material: One ball per group
Description: The players are positioned as the diagram indicates. The exercise consists of passing the ball and following the pass: A passes to B and goes to B's cone; B passes to D and goes to D's cone, etc.

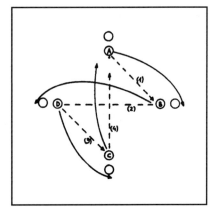

Objective: Short passes (various groups)
Difficulty: 4
No. of players: Various groups
Material: One ball per group
Description: Passes among A, B, C and D (support passes, in depth and side passes). A passes to B who returns it to him with a side pass, then to C who does the same and so on.

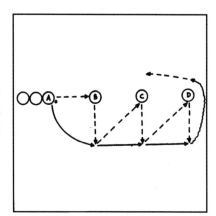

Objective: Short passes (various groups)
Difficulty: 3
No. of players: Various groups
Material: One ball per group
Description: The players are positioned in a circle and try to pass the ball in spite of the opposition of A who tries to intercept the ball.

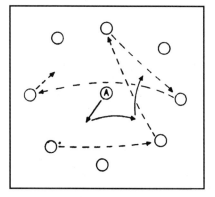

Objective: Short passes (various groups)
Difficulty: 4
No. of players: Various groups
Material: 4-5 balls and two cones per group
Description: Player B makes a pass to A and runs toward him. A returns it to him and B passes again to A who controls and makes a pass toward the cone so that B must run to receive it; from there he makes a pass to C who begins the exercise again from the other side.

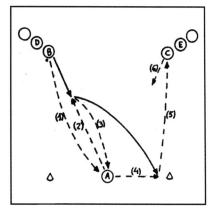

Objective: Short passes (various groups)
Difficulty: 3
No. of players: Various groups
Material: One ball per group
Description: All the players run freely throughout the field of play, each with an assigned number. At the coach's signal they must begin to pass the ball following the numerical order that have been assigned.

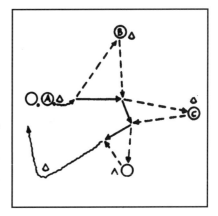

Objective: Short passes (various groups)
Difficulty: 3
No. of players: Various groups
Material: One ball and 5 cones per group
Description: Passes among players A,B,C, and D; player A passes to B and goes to the center, receives B's return pass and passes it to C. A receives the return from C and passes to D, receives the return from D and dribbles back to the starting point while the next player in line is making the run.

Long passes
Exercises with groups of 2

Objective: Long passes (between 2 players)
Difficulty: 2
No. of players: Groups of 2
Material: One ball and two cones per group
Description: Players A and B are positioned 30 yards apart and exchange long passes, playing with all the contact surfaces.

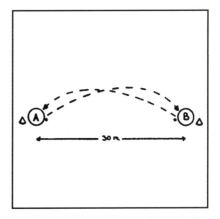

Objective: Long passes (between 2 players)
Difficulty: 2
No. of players: Groups of 2
Material: One ball and one goal per group
Description: The players are positioned on either side of the goal and make long passes back and forth over the goal.

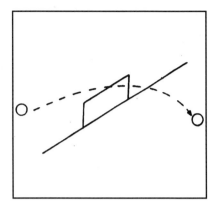

Objective: Long passes (between 2 players)
Difficulty: 4
No. of players: Groups of 2
Material: One ball per group
Description: Players A and B are positioned some 5 yards from their respective goals and exchange long shots, trying to score. They cannot move backwards to defend the shot.

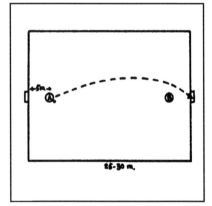

Objective: Long passes (between 2 players)
Difficulty: 3
No. of players: Groups of 2
Material: One ball and two zones per group
Description: Players A and B pass the ball between themselves trying to make it land within his teammate's square. Each good shot gets one point.

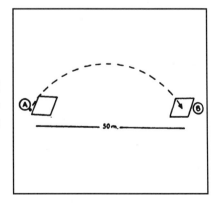

Objective: Long passes (between 2 players)
Difficulty: 3
No. of players: Groups of 2
Material: One ball and one zone per group
Description: Players A and B try to place the ball by means of a long pass within a marked zone located at some 25-30 yards. Each good shot gets one point.

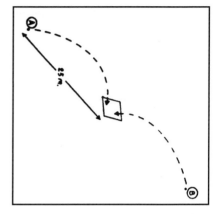

Objective: Long passes (between 2 players)
Difficulty: 3
No. of players: Groups of 2
Material: One ball and two flags/markers per group
Description: The player in possession of the ball makes a pass to his teammate located on the other side of the posts. The ball cannot pass between the posts, but rather must make a parabolic trajectory.

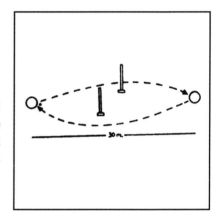

Objective: Long passes (between 2 players)
Difficulty: 3
No. of players: Groups of 2
Material: Two balls and two cones per group
Description: Players A and B simultaneously exchange long passes. They each receive the pass, leave it and sprint to the opposite side to repeat the exercise.

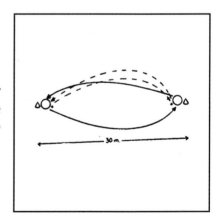

Objective: Long passes (between 2 players)
Difficulty: 3
No. of players: Groups of 2
Material: One ball and 4 cones per group
Description: Player A passes the ball to B and runs toward the cone located on his diagonal, where he will receive the pass from B. After making the pass, B goes to the cone located on his diagonal to receive a pass from A, etc.

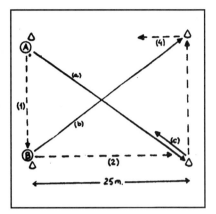

Objective: Long passes (between 2 players)
Difficulty: 3
No. of players: Groups of 2
Material: One ball per group
Description: Player A passes the ball to his teammate B located about 30 yards away, who receives it and makes a self pass and returns the ball to A to repeat the action.

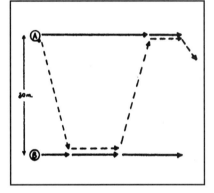

Objective: Long passes (between 2 players)
Difficulty: 3
No. of players: Groups of 2
Material: One ball per group
Description: Players A and B are positioned 30 yards apart and run parallel through the field of play exchanging passes. Play with all surface contacts.

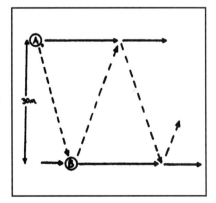

Exercises with groups of 3

Objective: Long passes (between 2 players)
Difficulty: 3
No. of players: Groups of 3
Material: One ball per group
Description: Player A passes the ball to B over the goal and runs to occupy his place.

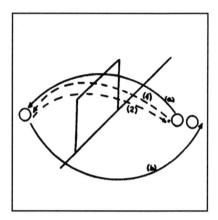

Objective: Long passes (among 3 players)
Difficulty: 3
No. of players: Groups of 3
Material: One ball per group
Description: Player A passes to C who from the center of the field tries to score on the goal defended by B who is positioned at the top of the area. B cannot retreat to his goal until C has kicked the ball.

Objective: Long passes (among 3 players)
Difficulty: 4
No. of players: Groups of 3
Material: One ball, 3 cones and 3 flags/markers per group
Description: Players A, B, and C pass the ball without letting it pass over or touch the flags. They must pass around the flags with a curving trajectory.

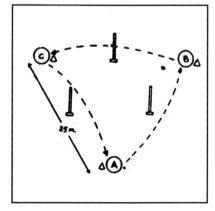

Objective: Long passes (among 3 players)
Difficulty: 3
No. of players: Groups of 3
Material: One ball and 4 cones per group
Description: Players A and B, positioned on the area lines try to pass the ball in spite of the opposition of C who plays as a goalie, trying to intercept the ball with his hands.

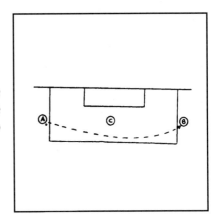

Objective: Long passes (among 3 players)
Difficulty: 3
No. of players: Groups of 3
Material: One ball and 4 cones per group
Description: Each player makes a pass following a pre-established order. After each pass the passer runs to occupy the cone opposite to the one where he sent the pass.

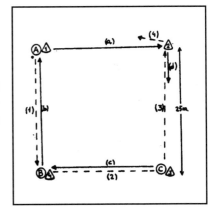

Objective: Long passes (among 3 players)
Difficulty: 3
No. of players: Groups of 3
Material: One ball and 3 cones per group
Description: Player B moves toward the cone occupied by player C. On the way, he receives a pass from A then dribbles around the cone and returns the pass to A. A passes into the run of C who is moving toward the cone vacated by B and C repeats the exercise and so on.

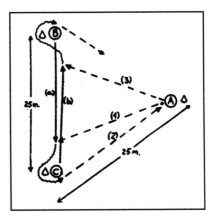

Objective: Long passes (among 3 players)
Difficulty: 3
No. of players: Groups of 3
Material: One ball and 6 cones per group
Description: Player A dribbles from cone X up to cone Y, where he makes a pass to B. He then returns to cone X to wait for the next pass. B does the same action with C and C with A, etc.

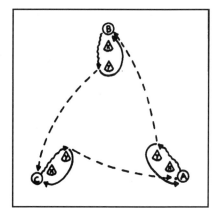

Objective: Long passes (among 3 players)
Difficulty: 3
No. of players: Groups 3
Material: One ball per group
Description: Players A, B and C run in a parallel form through the field of play. A makes a pass to B and runs to take his place; B dribbles up to the center and makes a pass to C for him to repeat the same movement.

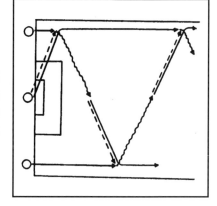

Objective: Long pass (among 3 players)
Difficulty: 3
No. of players: Groups of 3
Material: One ball per group
Description: Players A, B and C run in a parallel form through the field of play. B makes a pass to A and A returns it to him: B from his side position crosses the ball to C who then plays toward the center for A who returns it to him and C crosses for B and the exercise continues.

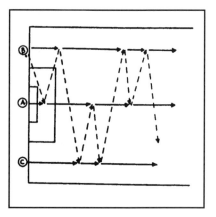

Objective: Long passes (among 3 players)
Difficulty: 3
No. of players: Groups of 3
Material: One ball per group
Description: Passes among players A, B and C; with six passes they must run through the whole field of play.

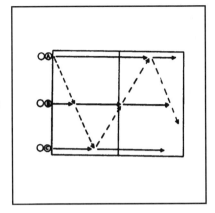

Objective: Long passes (among 4 players)
Difficulty: 3
No. of players: Groups of 4
Material: Two balls and 4 cones per group
Description: Players A and B pass the ball diagonally toward their teammates C and D. C and D then make frontal passes toward A and B to begin the exercise again.

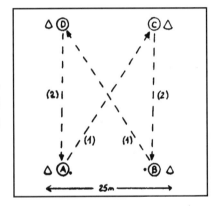

Objective: Long passes (among 4 players)
Difficulty: 3
No. of players: Groups of 4
Material: One ball and 4 cones per group
Description: Round of passes among the players; A makes a pass to B, B passes to C and C to D who returns it to B and B sends it toward A to begin the exercise again.

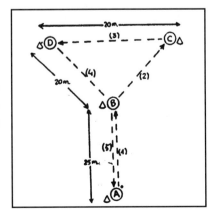

Objective: Long passes (among 4 players)
Difficulty: 3
No. of players: Groups of 4
Material: One ball and 4 cones per group
Description: The distribution of the players is similar to the previous exercise. Each player receives and passes to the same player. B makes a pass to C and he receives from C to pass to D.

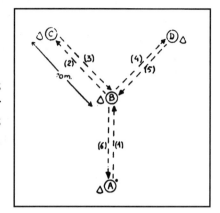

Objective: Long passes (among 4 passes)
Difficulty: 3
No. of players: Groups of 4
Material: One ball and 4 cones per group
Description: Players pass the ball according to the order of the letters; A passes to B, B to C, C to D and D again to A.

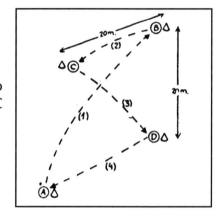

Objective: Long passes (among 4 players)
Difficulty: 3
No. of players: Groups of 4
Material: Two balls and 4 cones per group
Description: Players A and B pass the ball to teammates C and D; they exchange their positions and receive the return pass from the same player.

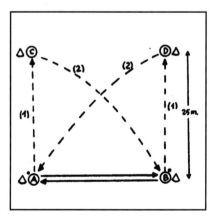

Objective: Long passes (among 4 players)
Difficulty: 3
No. of players: Groups of 4
Material: One ball per group
Description: Player A sends the ball toward B and runs to circle the center cone. Player B receives the pass from A, passes the ball to C and goes around the center cone.

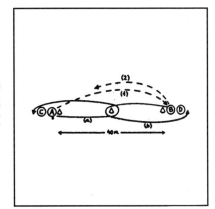

Objective: Long passes (among 4 players)
Difficulty: 3
No. of players: Groups of 4
Material: Two balls and 5 cones per group
Description: Player A passes to his teammate C while B does the same with D. A and B, after making the pass, exchange their positions going around the center cone; in their new positions they receive passes from C and D respectively.

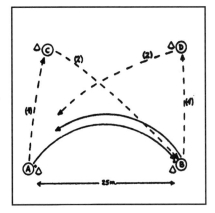

Objective: Long passes (among 4 players)
Difficulty: 3
No. of players: Groups of 4
Material: One ball and 4 cones per group
Description: Player A makes successive passes to B, C and D, who return them first time. Players B, C and D, after returning the pass, go to the cone on their right. A also moves to the right after the last pass to D. The action may be repeated on the opposite side.

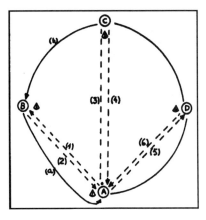

Objective: Long passes (among 4 players)
Difficulty: 3
No. of players: Groups of 4
Material: One ball per group and 3 cones
Description: Passes among players A, B, C, D located in a triangular formation; after each pass the player follows the ball to take the place of the teammate to whom he has passed.

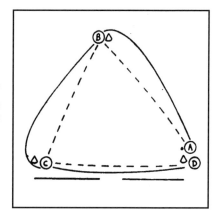

Objectivity: Long passes (among 4 players)
Difficulty: 3
No. of players: Groups of 4
Material: One ball per group and 4 cones
Description: Player A passes the ball to B, B to C. C must meet the ball halfway through his run toward the cone, dribble up to circle the cone and from there pass on to A who will begin the exercise again, this time with player D.

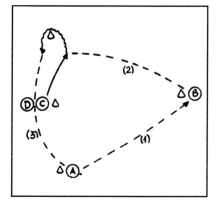

Objectivity: Long passes (among 4 players)
Difficulty: 3
No. of players: Groups of 4
Material: Two balls per group and 4 cones
Description: Round of passes among players who are located at the cones; A makes successive passes to B, C, and D who return the ball first time.

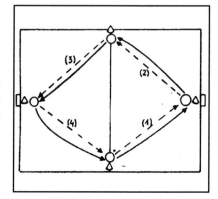

Exercises with various groups

Objectivity: Long passes (various groups)
Difficulty: 3
No. of players: Various groups
Material: One ball per group
Description: Player A sends the ball alternately to B, C and D, who return the ball to A. The players must remain stationary, maintaining the distances between them.

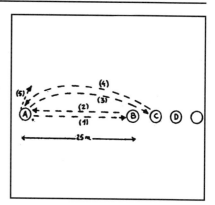

Objective: Long passes (various groups)
Difficulty: 3
No. of players: Various groups
Material: 2-3 balls per group
Description: Passes among the players who are located at the cones. They play with two balls; passes start from cones 1 and 5 and continue around as in the diagram.

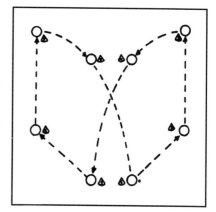

Objective: Long passes (groups)
Difficulty: 3
No. of players: Various groups
Material: Two balls per group
Description: Players A and B return the passes of their teammates X and Y who are located at the corners; A and B are continuously turning to meet the next ball.

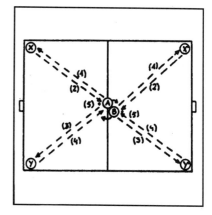

Objective: Long passes (various groups)
Difficulty: 3
No. of players: Various groups
Material: 3-4 balls and 5-6 cones per group
Description: Passing, receiving and dribbling (give and go's) among players A, B, C and D with stationary players X. Player A sends the ball to the first player X who returns it first time, leading A so that he receives the ball in stride. When A reaches the next cone, he performs another wall pass with the next X and so on. The next player starts when the player ahead reaches the 2nd cone.

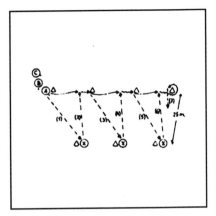

Objective: Long passes (various groups)
Difficulty: 3
No. of players: Various groups
Material: 4-5 balls and 6 cones per group
Description: Round of passes between the players located at the cones; after each pass the passer follows the ball to take position at the cone he passed to.

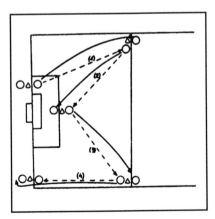

Objective: Long passes (various groups)
Difficulty: 3
No. of players: Various groups
Material: 2-3 ball and 5 cones per group
Description: Round of passes between the players located at the cones; after each pass the passer follows the ball to take position at the cone he passed to.

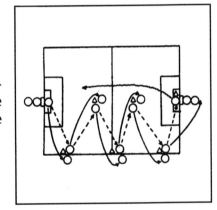

Objective: Long passes (various groups)
Difficulty: 3
No. of players: Various groups
Material: 2-3 balls and 6 cones per group
Description: Round of passes between the players located at the cones; after each pass the passer follows the ball to take position at the cone he passed to.

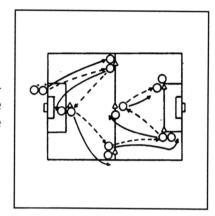

Objective: Long passes (various groups)
Difficulty: 3
No. of players: Various groups
Material: 2-3 balls and 4 cones per group
Description: Round of passes among the players located at the cones; after each pass the passer follows the pass to take position at the cone he passed to. At the last cone there will be a defender who will fight with the offense to prevent the offense from receiving the pass from C.

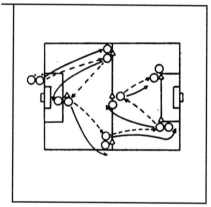

Objective: Long passes (various groups)
Difficulty: 3
No. of players: Various groups
Material: Two balls and 6 cones per group
Description: Round of passes between the players located at the cones; after each pass the passer follows the ball to take position at the cone he passed to. They play simultaneously on both sides; A passes to B who dribbles and passes to C who dribbles and passes to D.

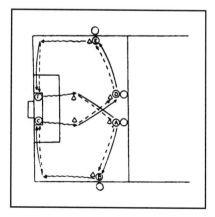

Objective: Long passes (various groups)
Difficulty: 4
No. of players: Various groups
Material: 3-4 balls and 5 cones per group
Description: Round of passes between the players located at the cones; after each pass the passer follows the ball to take position at the cone he passed to. A passes to B who intersects toward C; C plays with D who supports C again so that C intersects again toward B.

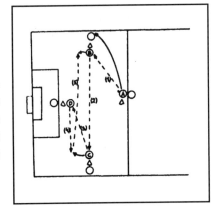

Objective: Long passes (various groups)
Difficulty: 3
No. of players: Various groups
Material: 4 balls and 4 cones per group
Description: The 4 players dribble the ball from the goal line up to the cone and make a pass on the diagonal; when they control their teammate's pass they return to the starting point.

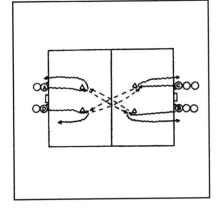

Objective: Long passes (various groups)
Difficulty: 3
No. of players: Various groups
Material: 4 balls and 4 cones per group
Description: The 4 players dribble the ball from the goal line up to the cone and make a pass on the diagonal; when they control their teammate's pass they go to the starting point of the next group.

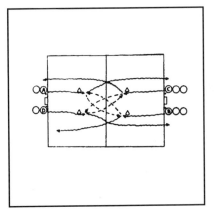

Objective: Long passes (various groups)
Difficulty: 3
No. of players: Various groups
Material: 4 ball per group
Description: The diagram indicates the players' locations; player A sends a pass to D who dribbles and makes a side pass for A who shoots on goal. At the same time C and B do the same exercise.

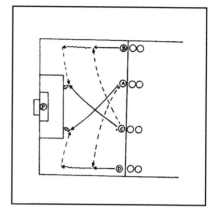

Objective: Long passes (various groups)
Difficulty: 3
No. of players: Various groups
Material: One ball and two hurdles
Description: Players exchange passes between the hurdles. After each pass, the player who made the pass must go to the other group, jumping over the hurdle.

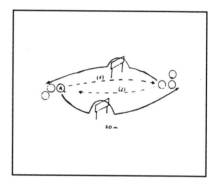

Passes according to contact surface

Objective: Passes-contact surfaces
Difficulty: 2
No. of players: Groups of 2
Material: One ball and 6 cones
Description: Player A passes the ball to B without touching any cone in his path. Use the inside of the foot for accuracy.

Objective: Passes-contact surfaces
Difficulty: 2
No. of players: Groups of 3
Material: One ball per group
Description: Player A passes the ball to B. The ball must pass between C's legs. Use the inside of the foot for accuracy.

Objective: Passes-contact surfaces
Difficulty: 3
No. of players: Groups of 2
Material: One ball and one hoop per group
Description: Use the inner instep. Player A passes the ball to B. The ball must pass through the hoop.

Objective: Passes-contact surfaces
Difficulty: 3
No. of players: Groups of 2
Material: One ball and one cone per group
Description: Use the inner instep. Player A passes the ball to B. The ball must pass around the cone.

Objective: Passes-contact surfaces
Difficulty: 3
No. of players: Groups of 3
Material: One ball and 3 cones per group
Description: Use the outer instep. The players pass the ball among themselves, dodging the cones with curving passes.

Objective: Passes-contact surfaces
Difficulty: 3
No. of players: Groups of 3
Material: One ball and 4 cones per group
Description: Use the entire instep. The players pass the ball among themselves trying to make the ball pass between the cones.

Objective: Passes-contact surfaces
Difficulty: 3
No. of players: Groups of 2
Material: One ball and one hurdle per group
Description: Use the entire instep. The players pass the ball among themselves trying to make the ball pass over the hurdle.

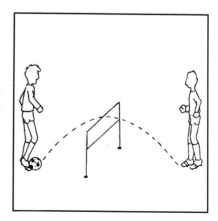

Objective: Passes-contact surfaces
Difficulty: 3
No. of players: Groups of 2
Material: One ball per group
Description: Player A sends the ball toward C who makes a pass to his teammate B with a heel pass.

Objective: Passes-contact surfaces
Difficulty: 3
No. of players: Groups of 3
Material: One ball per group
Description: Player A sends the ball to B who after control of the ball makes a heel pass to his teammate A, who has made a run to go after the return pass.

Objective: Passes-contact surfaces
Difficulty: 3
No. of players: Groups of 2
Material: One ball per group
Description: Use the entire instep. Player A sends the ball to B with volley and half-volley passes.

Objective: Passes-contact surfaces
Difficulty: 3
No. of players: Groups of 2
Material: One ball and one hurdle per group
Description: Use the entire instep. Players A and B pass the ball back and forth with volley and half-volley passes over a hurdle.

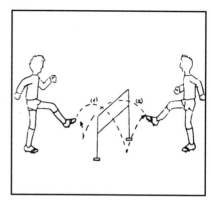

Wall passes

Objective: Wall passes
Difficulty: 3
No. of players: Groups of 3
Material: One ball and 4 cones per group
Description: Player A dribbles the ball and must avoid the defender C by means of a wall pass with B within the area marked off by the 4 cones.

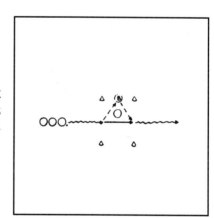

Objective: Wall passes
Difficulty: 3
No. of players: Groups of 3
Material: One ball and 4 cones per group
Description: Players A and B play together to get past the opposition of X. They can only shoot after having made a wall pass.

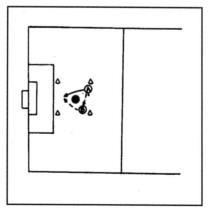

Objective: Wall passes
Difficulty: 3
No. of players: Various groups
Material: One ball per group
Description: Team X faces team Y; players A and B only work with the team in possession of the ball and only to make the wall pass.

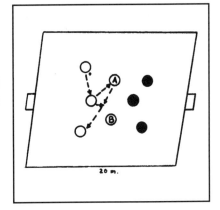

Objective: Wall passes
Difficulty: 3
No. of players: Various groups
Material: One ball and 6 cones per group
Description: Player A dribbles the ball and at each cone makes a wall pass with the player at the opposition cone.

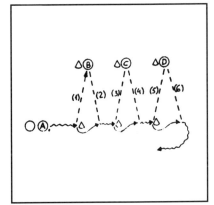

Objective: Wall passes
Difficulty: 3
No. of players: Groups of 3
Material: One ball and two cones per group
Description: Player A passes the ball to B, turns and runs in the opposite direction where he receives the return pass from B. A dribbles the ball to the other cone and repeats the same move with C.

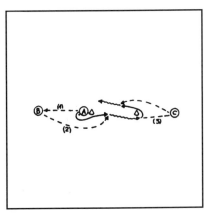

Objective: Wall passes
Difficulty: 3
No. of players: Various groups
Material: 1One ball per group
Description: On a 10 x 10 surface, players X and Y play 1 v 1 with the support of the 4 stationary players who are located on the perimeter of the area.

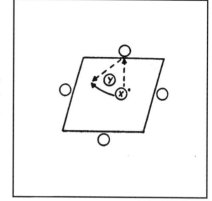

Objective: Wall passes
Difficulty: 3
No. of players: Various groups
Material: One ball per group
Description: Two teams play to score between the cones, but they cannot shoot on goal without having first made a wall pass that facilitates the touch.

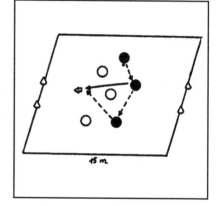

Objective: Wall passes
Difficulty: 3
No of players: Groups of 2
Material: One ball per group
Description: Player A dribbles the ball with his teammate B running behind him at some distance. When he arrives at the opposing cone he steps on the ball with the sole of his foot and pushes it toward B, who makes an air pass towards A's path so that he can get the ball again and repeat the same action.

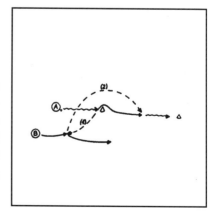

Objective: Wall passes
Difficulty: 3
No. of players: Various groups
Material: One ball per group
Description: Two teams play to score in the opponent's goal but may not shoot unless they first make a wall pass with one of the their two stationary teammates positioned on either side of the goal.

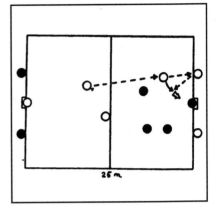

Objective: Wall passes
Difficulty: 3
No of players: Various groups
Material: One ball per group
Description: Two teams play to score in the opponent's goal: each team has two stationary players located on the sides of the field who the players use for wall passes to avoid the opposition.

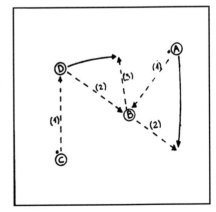

Objective: Wall passes
Difficulty: 3
No. of players: Groups of 4
Material: Two balls per group
Description: Player A plays a wall pass with player B, who turns and plays a wall pass with player D.

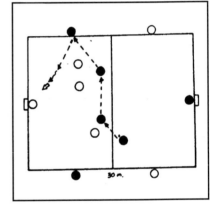

Objective: Wall passes
Difficulty: 3
No. of players: Groups of 3
Material: One ball per group
Description: Player A makes a pass to player B and B plays a wall pass with player C. Then player B passes the ball to player A to begin the exercise again.

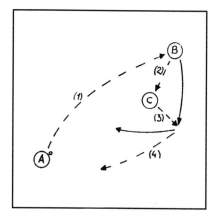

Objective: Wall passes
Difficulty: 3
No. of players: Groups of 3
Material: One ball per group
Description: Player A makes a pass to player B and B plays a wall pass with player D to avoid the opposition from player X. Then player B passes the ball to player A to begin the exercise again, this time with player C.

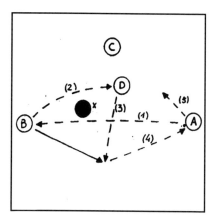

Application plays

Objective: Pass application plays
Difficulty: 3
No. of players: Various groups
Material: One ball per group
Description: Players are distributed in two teams, each player has a ball. Each team tries to make the greatest number of passes in a determined amount of time. The team who makes the most passes wins. Rival players can intercept the ball.

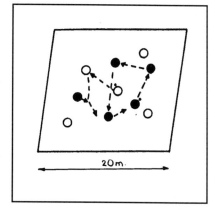

Objection: Pass application plays
Difficulty: 3
No. of players: Various groups
Material: One ball per player
Description: The group of three players must return the passes from their teammates. The condition is that the pass may not be returned to the same player who passed it. The player who has committed the least number of errors in returning passes wins at the end of the established time.

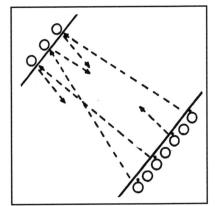

Objective: Pass application plays
Difficulty: 3
No. of players: Various groups
Material: One ball per group
Description: Players pass the ball among themselves. The coach counts silently to 50, saying the tens out loud. The player who is holding the ball when a "ten" is announced is eliminated. The winner is the last player to be eliminated.

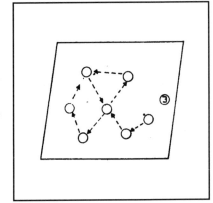

Objective: Pass application plays
Difficulty: 3
No. of players: Various groups
Material: One ball per group
Description: The players of each team try to make the greatest number of passes without the opposing team taking the ball. Each time a team makes ten passes, one point is scored. The team who has scored the most points in a certain time wins.

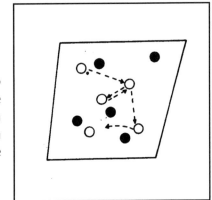

Objective: Pass application plays
Difficulty: 3
No. of players: Various groups
Material: One ball per group
Description: Players of each team must try to dribble the ball over the lines that limit the playing surface. Each team tries to go after, by means of passes, the most favorable situation so that one of the members manages to exit the playing field dribbling the ball.

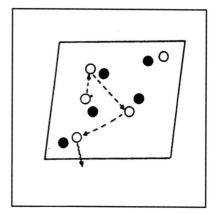

Objective: Pass application plays
Difficulty: 3
No. of players: Various groups
Material: One ball per group
Description: Players of each team pass the ball among themselves within their field of play. The team who has made the least amount of passing errors, according to the coach's criteria, is the winner.

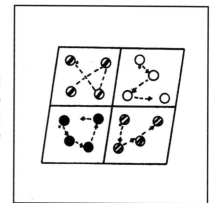

Objective: Pass application plays
Difficulty: 3
No. of players: Various groups
Material: One ball per group
Description: Players of each team pass the ball among themselves within their field of play. The team that has made the most passes in a determined time frame is the winner.

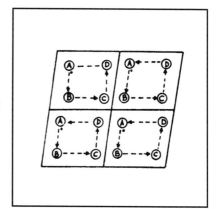

Objective: Pass application plays
Difficulty: 3
No. of players: Various groups
Material: One ball per group
Description: Players of each team pass the ball among themselves within their field of play. Another team readies (prepares) their players to run, one by one, a determined distance. The team who makes the most passes is the winner. Playing time: the time that each running team takes to run the distance.

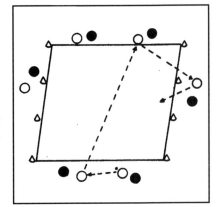

Objective: Pass application plays
Difficulty: 3
No. of players: Various groups
Material: One ball per group
Description: Location of players is indicated in the diagram. Each team tries to score a goal in the goals located at both sides of the field. The goal is only valid if it is scored from outside toward the inside of the field of play.

Objective: Pass application plays
Difficulty: 3
No. of players: Various groups
Material: One ball and a cone per group
Description: Players located on the outside of the circle pass the ball among themselves, so that they find the most favorable situation to try to hit the center cone, defended by another player.

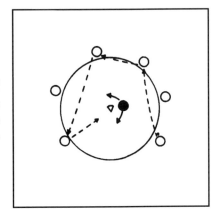

Objective: Pass application plays
Difficulty: 3
No. of players: Various groups
Material: One ball per group
Description: Players located on the outside of the play zone pass the ball among themselves with a determined number of touches. The players located within the square try to intercept the ball.

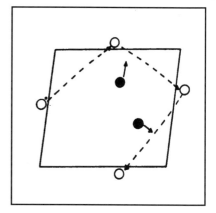

Objective: Pass application plays
Difficulty: 3
No. of players: Various groups
Material: One ball per group
Description: The players, each one located in a corresponding grid (square) pass the ball with a determined number of touches. Player X tries to intercept the ball, moving throughout the entire space.

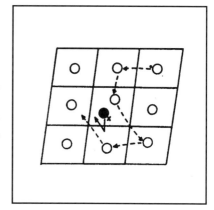

Objective: Pass application plays
Difficulty: 3
No. of players: Various groups
Material: One ball per group
Description: Players 1, 2, and 3 try to pass the ball in order. Each time they do it they win a point. Player X tries to prevent it.

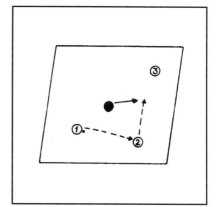

Objective: Pass application plays
Difficulty: 3
No. of players: Various groups
Material: One ball per group
Description: Players of team Y pass the ball among themselves outside of the circle, in hopes of creating an opportune moment to pass toward the inner part of the circle, defended by team X. Each time that the ball arrives in this circle, team Y gets a point. Exchange roles after a set time. The team with the most points wins.

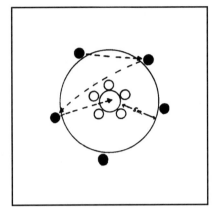

Objective: Pass application plays
Difficulty: 3
No. of players: Various groups
Material: One ball per group
Description: The players positioned in rows as in the diagram pass the ball successively to the stationary player and go to the end of the line. The team who makes the most passes in a determined time wins.

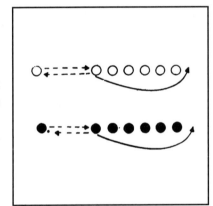

Objective: Pass application plays
Difficulty: 3
No. of players: Various groups
Material: One ball per group
Description: The players of the team in possession of the ball pass the ball to try to touch a player of the opposing team. The touched player is eliminated. The team who eliminates all the players of the opposing team first wins.

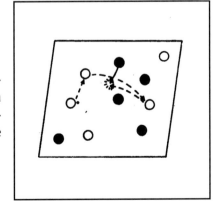

Objective: Pass application plays
Difficulty: 3
No. of players: Various groups
Material: One ball per group
Description: The players in the grids (squares)
pass the ball among themselves. When one of
them makes a bad pass, he goes to grid D and
the rest advance one square. If D makes a bad
pass, he exchanges his position with the outside player. The player who manages to stay
longest in grid A wins.

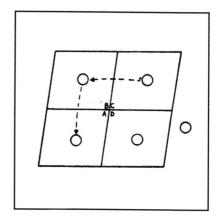

Objective: Pass application plays
Difficulty: 3
No. of players: Various groups
Material: One ball per group
Description: Soccer-squash court: the players
play against the wall as in a game of squash.
They must avoid the line marked on the wall
and must play the first touch. Two contacts are
allowed only if the controlling touch is made
with the chest or the head.

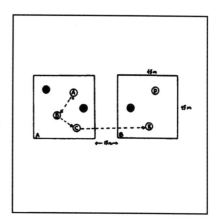

Objective: Pass application plays
Difficulty: 3
No. of players: Various groups
Material: One ball per group
Description: Play of short passes. Players A, B,
and C try to play the ball among themselves in
spite of the presence of the X defenders. After
the fifth pass, they go after the pass from their
teammates D and E. The X defenders try to
intercept. The exercise is repeated through players D and E.

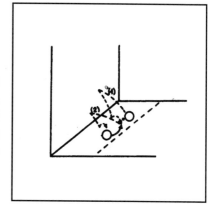

Objective: Pass application plays
Difficulty: 3
No. of players: Various groups
Material: One ball per group
Description: Play of short passes. Players A, B, and C try to play the ball among themselves in spite of the presence of the X defenders. After the fifth pass, they go after the pass to their teammates D, E, and F. The X defenders try to intercept. The exercise is repeated through players D, E, and F.

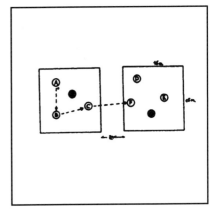

Objective: Pass application plays
Difficulty: 3
No. of players: Various groups
Material: One ball per group
Description: Players X and Y alternately kick the ball against the bench with the first touch. The object of the play is to make the ball, after bouncing off the bench, pass over the back line where it can't be returned by the other player. Each time this happens a point is scored.

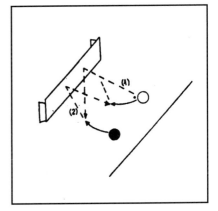

Objective: Pass application plays
Difficulty: 3
No. of players: Various groups
Material: One ball per group
Description: The diagram indicates the position of the players. In each zone two teams of two players each play for possession and look for the chance to pass to the adjacent zone.

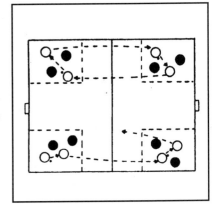

Objective: Pass application plays
Difficulty: 3
No. of players: Various groups
Material: One ball per group
Description: The diagram indicates the position of the players. In each zone two teams of two players each play for possession and look for the chance to pass to the diagonally opposite zone.

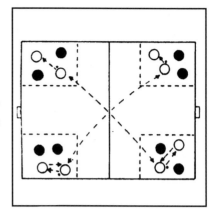

Objective: Pass application plays
Difficulty: 3
No. of players: Various groups
Material: Two balls per group
Description: Player A sends a long pass to B who at the first touch passes to C; B moves toward C's location; player C dribbles to occupy B's location; The exercise is repeated with D passing to E and E to the center for B etc.

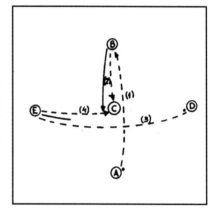

Objective: Pass application plays
Difficulty: 3
No. of players: Various groups
Material: One ball per group
Description: 3 Y players vs. 2 X players; the attackers (Y) can only move into the 2nd zone dribbling through one of the two small goals located at both sides of the field; if they get to the 2nd zone, they face two other defenders who try to prevent them from moving to the 3rd zone. When they are beaten, defenders from the 1st zone go to zone 3.

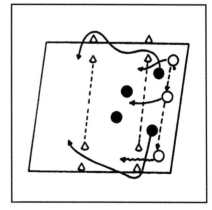

Objective: Pass application plays
Difficulty: 3
No. of players: Various groups
Material: One ball per group
Description: The players make passes from a distance of 30 yards into a grid marked with cones. Each zone has a value and points are scored according to where the first bounce lands.

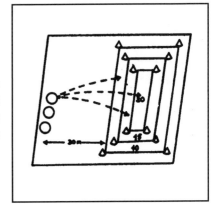

Objective: Pass application plays
Difficulty: 3
No. of players: Various groups
Material: One ball per group
Description: Two teams face each other playing tennis soccer; each player can only touch the ball once and the team 3 times. The third contact must send the ball to the opponent's side. There is no net, only a neutral zone that penalizes if the ball touches in it.

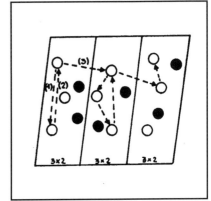

Objective: Pass application plays
Difficulty: 3
No. of players: Various groups
Material: One ball per group
Description: The diagram indicates the position of the players. In each zone are 3 attackers and 2 defenders. Play starts in the first zone with the attackers looking for the opening to pass the ball to a teammate in the 2nd zone. When the ball moves to the 2nd zone, the attackers there try to get the ball to a teammate in the 3rd zone and so on.

Objective: Pass application plays
Difficulty: 3
No. of players: Various groups
Material: One ball per group
Description: The diagram indicates the position of the players. Play 4 v 2 with the two attackers in each of the outside zones and the two defenders in the inside zone. The players in the outside zones try to pass the ball to their teammates in the opposite zone while the defenders try to intercept. Passes must be on the ground.

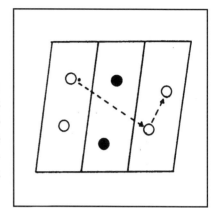

Objective: Pass application plays
Difficulty: 3
No. of players: Various groups
Material: One ball per group
Description: The diagram indicates the starting position of the players. In each zone 3 v 2 is played, starting in zone 1. The team in possession makes passes to create an opportunity to pass to a teammate in the 2nd zone. When the ball is sent to the 2nd zone, the player who passed the ball moves to join his teammates in that zone. 3 v 2 continues in zone 2 until the pass is made to zone 3 and the exercise continues.

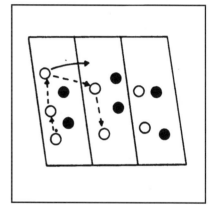

Objective: Pass application plays
Difficulty: 3
No. of players: Various groups
Material: One ball per group
Description: The diagram indicates the position of the players. The team in possession tries to play the ball with first time passes and at the correct time pass the ball to their teammates in the 2nd zone who in turn do the same, trying to pass to the 3rd zone.

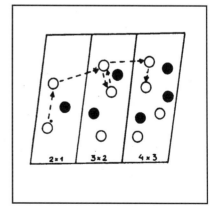

Objective: Pass application plays
Difficulty: 3
No. of players: Various groups
Material: One ball per group
Description: The diagram indicates the position of the players. The team in possession tries to play the ball with first time passes and at the correct time pass the ball to their teammates in the 2nd zone; if 5 passes are made in the 1st zone, the player who passes into the 2nd zone moves into the 2nd zone and the same for the 2nd zone. If it is possible, a long pass can be made between the 1st and 3rd zone.

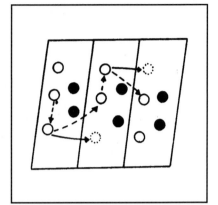

Objective: Pass application plays
Difficulty: 3
No. of players: Various groups
Material: One ball per group
Description: The diagram indicates the position of the players. The team in possession tries to play the ball with first time passes and at the correct time pass the ball to their teammate in the 2nd zone; this one in turn tries to get the pass to his teammates in the 3rd zone.

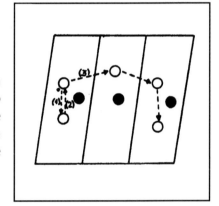

Objective: Pass application plays
Difficulty: 3
No. of players: Various groups
Material: One ball per group
Description: The diagram indicates the player's positions. Each team tries to pass the ball to the stationary player; only first time passes are permitted. Each time a team manages to get the ball to the stationary player a point is scored.

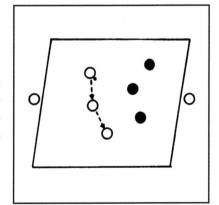

Objective: Pass application plays
Difficulty: 3
No. of players: Various groups
Material: One ball per group
Description: In a reduced field 4 x 4 is played; a goal does not count if the pass doesn't come from marked zones in the corners.

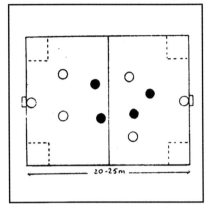

Objective: Pass application plays
Difficulty: 3
No. of players: Various groups
Material: One ball per group
Description: A team of 4 players (2 defenders who can't move into the offensive zone and two attackers who can't move into the defensive zone) face a team of 2 players where one is offensive and the other defensive.

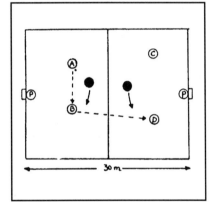

Objective: Pass application plays
Difficulty: 3
No. of players: Various groups
Material: One ball and 6-8 cones per group
Description: Two teams face each other; the objective is to touch, with the ball, as many cones as possible. Each time a ball touches a cone a point is won.

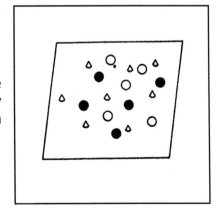

Objective: Pass application plays
Difficulty: 3
No. of players: Various groups
Material: One ball per group
Description: Two teams face each other freely; only goals scored after a back pass are counted.

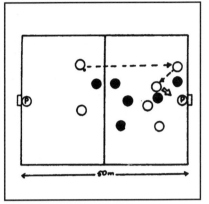

Objective: Pass application plays
Difficulty: 3
No. of players: Various groups
Material: One ball and 8 cones per group
Description: The diagram indicates the player's positions. The outside players must pass the ball until they find the ideal moment to shoot to the inside zone defended by goalie P.

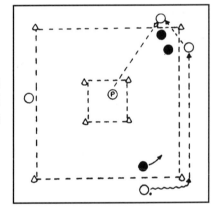

CHAPTER 4
RECEIVING THE BALL
Exercises for movement mechanics

Objective: Movement mechanics
Difficulty: 2
No. of players: Groups of 2
Material: One ball per pair
Description: Player A shoots toward goal so that player B must make the save, control the ball and return it to A to repeat the exercise.

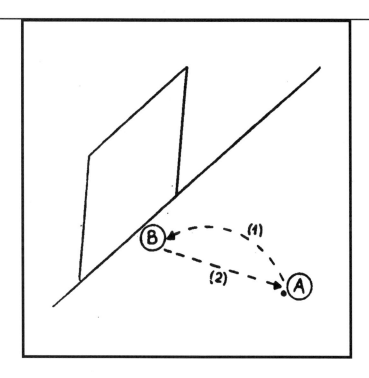

Objective: Movement mechanics
Difficulty: 2
No. of players: Groups of 3
Material: One ball per group
Description: Player C passes the ball alternately to players A and B, who return it to him. Before passing, all the players must stop the ball.

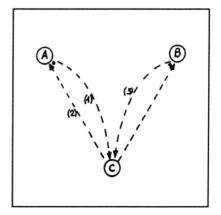

Objective: Movement mechanics
Difficulty: 2
No. of players: Groups of 5
Material: 4 balls per group
Description: Player A returns the ball successively to the players located around him, who pass it low. Before returning it, player A must stop the ball.

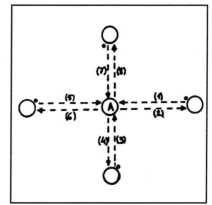

Objective: Movement mechanics
Difficulty: 3
No. of players: Groups of 5
Material: 4 balls per group
Description: Player A returns the ball successively to the players located around him, who make airborne passes. Before returning it, player A must stop the ball.

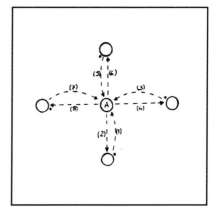

Objective: Movement mechanics
Difficulty: 3
No. of players: Various groups
Material: 4-5 balls per group
Description: Player A passes the ball to player C, who receives and dribbles toward B's position while B moves to take the place of A, who after making the pass goes to the end of the line.

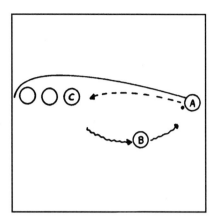

Objective: Movement mechanics
Difficulty: 4
No. of players: Groups of 3
Material: Two balls per group
Description: Player A receives and returns low passes that players B and C send to him alternately. Before going after a new pass, player A has to circle one of the cones located to his left and right.

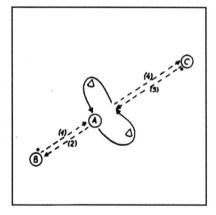

Objective: Movement mechanics
Difficulty: 4
No. of players: Groups of 3
Material: Two balls per group
Description: Player A receives and returns airborne passes that players B and C send to him alternately. Before going after a new pass, player A has to circle one of the cones located to his left and right.

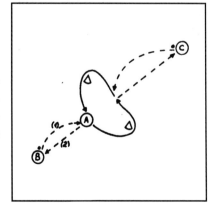

Objective: Movement mechanics
Difficulty: 4
No. of players: Groups of 3
Material: Two balls per group
Description: Player A, located between two cones, receives and returns the passes that players B and C send to him alternately. B and C make their pass before the ball arrives back to the other.

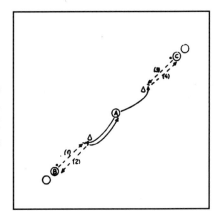

Exercises with different contact surfaces

Objective: Contact surfaces
Difficulty: 2
No. of players: Groups of 2
Material: One ball per group
Description: Player A throws the ball with his hands to player B to control with the sole of his foot.

Objective: Contact surfaces
Difficulty: 2
No. of players: One
Material: One ball per player
Description: The player throws the ball forward in the air with his hands and runs to settle it with his chest and dribble away.

Objective: Contact surfaces
Difficulty: 3
No. of players: Groups of 2
Material: One ball per group
Description: Player A throws the ball with his hands to player B who settles with his chest and returns the ball with a volley.

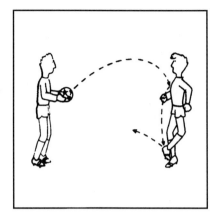

Objective: Contact surfaces
Difficulty: 3
No. of players: Groups of 2
Material: One ball per group
Description: Player B has his back to player A. Player A throws the ball with his hands to player B and says "Turn" to indicate the throw so B turns and receives it.

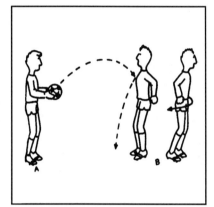

Objective: Contact surfaces
Difficulty: 3
No. of players: Groups of 2
Material: One ball per group
Description: Player A throws the ball with his hands to player B with a downward trajectory for B to receive on the bounce with either his chest or sole of the foot.

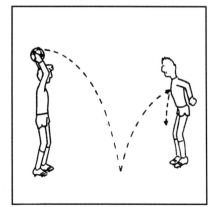

Objective: Contact surfaces
Difficulty: 3
No. of players: Groups of 2
Material: One ball per group
Description: Player A throws the ball with his hands to player B with a line drive trajectory for B to receive with the chest.

Objective: Contact surfaces
Difficulty: 3
No. of players: Groups of 2
Material: One ball per group
Description: Player A lobs the ball with his hands to player B who lets it bounce once and receives with his chest.

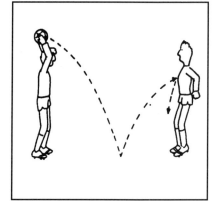

Objective: Contact surfaces
Difficulty: 4
No. of players: Groups of 3
Material: One ball per group
Description: Players are positioned in a triangular formation and pass the ball with their feet after receiving with the chest.

Objective: Contact surfaces
Difficulty: 4
No. of players: Groups of 2
Material: One ball per group
Description: Player A throws the ball with his hands to player B who takes it on one bounce, turns and dribbles away.

Objective: Contact surfaces
Difficulty: 4
No. of players: Groups of 2
Material: One ball per group
Description: Player A kicks the ball to player B who returns it first time and A gives a lofted pass to B who then turns, controls and dribbles away.

Objective: Contact surfaces
Difficulty: 3
No. of players: One
Material: One ball
Description: The player throws the ball in the air, runs and controls it with his thigh and dribbles away.

Objective: Contact surfaces
Difficulty: 3
No. of players: Groups of 2
Material: One ball per group
Description: Player A throws the ball to player B who receives with his thigh.

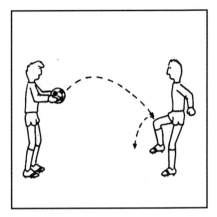

Objective: Contact surfaces
Difficulty: 4
No. of players: Groups of 2
Material: One ball per group
Description: Player A throws the ball with his hands to player B who is standing with his back to A and receives with his thigh.

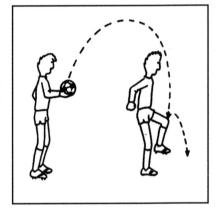

Objective: Contact surfaces
Difficulty: 1
No. of players: One
Material: One ball per player
Description: Player A throws the ball with his hands to player B who is standing with his back to A and receives with his foot.

Objective: Contact surfaces
Difficulty: 2
No. of players: Groups of 2
Material: One ball per group
Description: Player A throws the ball with his hands to player B, whose back is to him, and calls "Turn" to let B know that the pass is coming. B turns and receives with his foot.

Objective: Contact surfaces
Difficulty: 3
No. of players: One
Material: One ball per player
Description: The player throws the ball in the air with his hands backward over his head, turns and controls the ball with his foot.

Objective: Contact surfaces
Difficulty: 3
No. of players: Groups of 2
Material: One ball per group
Description: Player A throws the ball with his hands over the barrier to player B who receives with his foot, catches with his hands and throw the ball back to A who repeats the exercise.

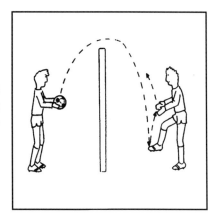

Objective: Contact surfaces
Difficulty: 4
No. of players: Groups of 2
Material: One ball per group
Description: Player A kicks the ball to player B who receives it with his foot and returns the pass to continue the exercise.

Objective: Contact surfaces
Difficulty: 4
No. of players: One
Material: One ball per player
Description: The player kicks the ball successively against the wall with the objective of receiving with the same foot each time the ball bounces.

Receiving while running

Objective: Receiving while running
Difficulty: 2
No. of players: One
Material: One ball per player
Description: The player rolls the ball forward with his hand (like a bowler), then runs after it to control it some yards further ahead.

Objective: Receiving while running
Difficulty: 2
No. of players: One
Material: One ball per player, one hurdle.
Description: The player throws the ball with his hands over the hurdle, then runs around the hurdle to receive it a few yards further up.

Objective: Receiving while running
Difficulty: 2
No. of players: One
Material: One ball per player, one hurdle.
Description: The player throws the ball with his hands over the hurdle, then runs after it, going under the hurdle, to receive it a few yards further up.

Objective: Receiving while running
Difficulty: 2
No. of players: Various groups
Material: One ball per group, one cone.
Description: Player A makes a ground pass toward the cone for player B to run onto. When B gets it, he dribbles around the cone and returns to the starting point.

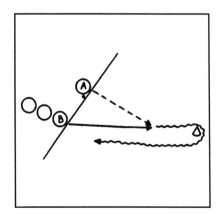

Objective: Receiving while running
Difficulty: 2
No. of players: Various groups
Material: One ball per group, one cone
Description: Player A makes an airborne pass toward the cone for player B to run onto. When B gets it, he dribbles around the cone and returns to the starting point.

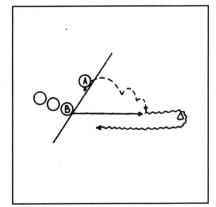

Objective: Receiving while running
Difficulty: Groups of 2
No. of players: Groups of 2
Material: One ball per group
Description: Player A throws the ball over player B, seated in front of him, and B gets up, turns and runs to receive it.

Objective: Receiving while running
Difficulty: 3
No. of players: Various groups
Material: 4-5 balls per group, 3 cones.
Description: Player A passes the ball toward the cone in front and player B runs to receive it before it reaches the cone. When B gets it, he dribbles to the opposite cone and the exercise is repeated on the other side.

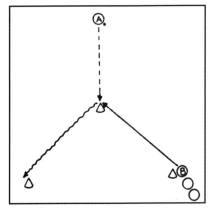

Objective: Receiving and running
Difficulty: 3
No. of players: Groups of 2
Material: One ball per group, one cone.
Description: Player A passes the ball toward the cone for player B to run onto. When B gets the ball, he turns and dribbles back to his starting position and repeats the exercise for A and so on.

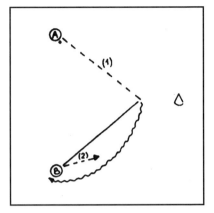

Objective: Receiving and running
Difficulty: 3
No. of players: Groups of 2
Material: One ball per group, 3 cones.
Description: Player A passes to player B, who passes toward the cone in front. Player A, after his pass, sprints in a straight line toward the pass of B, controls the ball and dribbles around the cone and back to his starting position. A then restarts the exercise for B and so on.

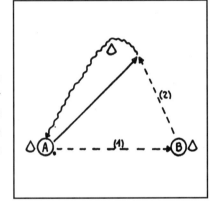

Objective: Receiving and running
Difficulty: 3
No. of players: Groups of 2
Material: One ball per group, 3 cones.
Description: Player X passes the ball toward the space between the cones in front so that player A runs onto it, controls and dribbles up to the cone (a); from there he passes to player X and returns to his starting position to repeat the exercise.

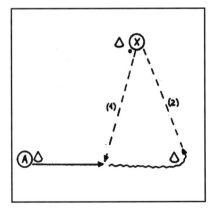

Objective: Receiving and running
Difficulty: 3
No. of players: Various groups
Material: One ball per group
Description: Player A passes the ball to player B and follows his pass. He circles B, who sends a ground pass into the return run of A who receives it and dribbles back to his starting position. A then hands off to the next player in line who repeats the exercise with the next B player.

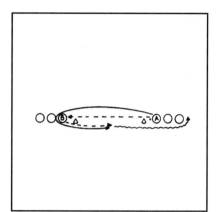

Objective: Receiving while running
Difficulty: 3
No. of players: Various groups
Material: One ball per group, 3 cones
Description: Player A dribbles some yards and passes the ball to player B, who receives it between cones 1-2 and dribbles to circle cone 3 up to cone 1. Player A, after making the pass runs toward cone 2 to begin the exercise again.

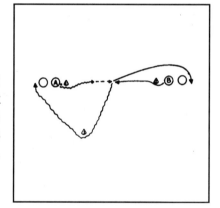

Objective: Receiving while running
Difficulty: 3
No. of players: Various groups
Material: One ball per group, 5 cones.
Description: Players A, C, E, and G pass a low ball toward the center cone; the low ball must be received by players B, D, F, and H respectively, before it arrives at said cone. When they receive it, they dribble back and return the ball to their teammate to repeat the pass.

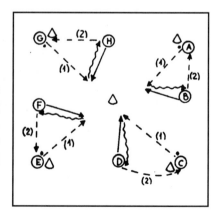

Objective: Receiving while running
Difficulty: 3
No. of players: Various groups
Material: One ball per group, 5 cones.
Description: Players A, C, E, and G pass an air-borne ball toward the center cone; the ball must be received by B, D, F, and H respectively, before it gets to said cone. When they receive it, they dribble back and return the ball to their team-mate to repeat the pass.

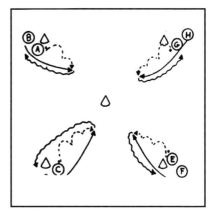

Objective: Receiving while running
Difficulty: 4
No. of players: Various groups
Material: Two balls per group, 6 cones.
Description: Player X receives the ball from player B halfway between 2 cones and dribbles up to the next cone, from which he makes a pass to D (who passes to B), goes around the cone and gets ready to receive a new pass from player C.

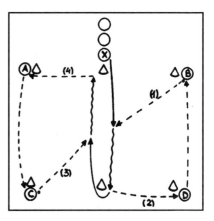

Objective: Receiving while running
Difficulty: 4
No. of players: Various groups
Material: 5 balls per group, 5 cones.
Description: Player A passes the ball so that player B gets it and dribbles up to the second cone. B leaves the ball and waits until player C passes a new ball to him to repeat the same exercise and so on at each cone.

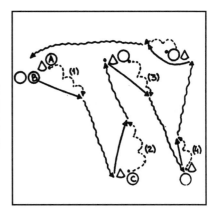

Objective: Receiving while running
Difficulty: 4
No. of players: Various groups
Material: One ball per group
Description: At each hurdle there is a stationary player who throws the balls over the hurdle. Player A runs after the ball that the stationary player throws, controls it and dribbles up to the next hurdle.

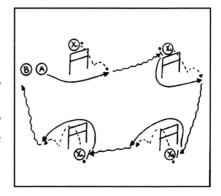

Change of direction while dribbling

Objective: Change of direction while dribbling
Difficulty: 2
No. of players: One
Material: One ball per player and several cones
Description: The players dribble the ball freely through the field of play; each time they come to a cone they step on the ball and dribble in the opposite direction.

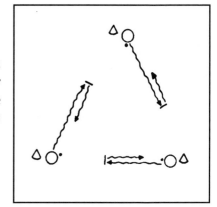

Objective: Change of direction while dribbling
Difficulty: 2
No. of players: One
Material: One ball per player and various cones
Description: Players run a course marked by cones; at each cone they must step on the ball to stop it and continue their dribble to the next cone and so on.

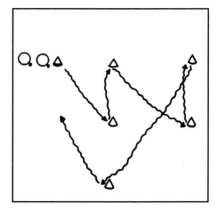

Objective: Change of direction while dribbling
Difficulty: 2
No. of players: One
Material: One ball per player
Description: Players run a course marked by cones; at each cone they must step on the ball to stop it and continue their dribble in a new direction according to the position of the opponent.

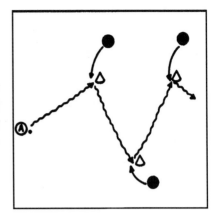

Receiving with opposition

Objective: Receiving with opposition
Difficulty: 3
No. of players: Groups of 4
Material: One ball per group
Description: C v D to try to win the ball passed by player A. The player that wins possession repeats the pass toward players A and B who try to get the ball and the exercise continues.

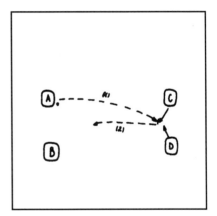

Objective: Receiving with opposition
Difficulty: 2
No. of players: Various groups
Material: One ball per group
Description: Players are located in two rows about 2 yards apart. Player C passes the ball toward one of the rows. The player who he passes to (here it is player B) must get to the ball quickly and control in spite of the opposition from A. After they receive, they send the ball again to C and go to the end of the line.

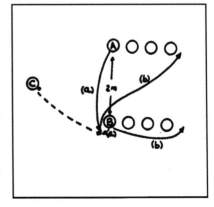

Objective: Receiving with opposition
Difficulty: 2
No. of players: Various groups
Material: Two balls per group
Description: X v Y to receive the ball that the players in the corners pass to them. Once they get the ball they must pass it to one of the two players who did not have the ball originally.

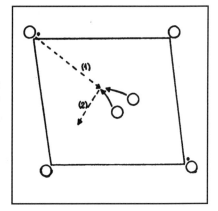

Objective: Receiving with opposition
Difficulty: 3
No. of players: Various groups
Material: 4 ball per group
Description: A v X to receive the ball that the players in the corners pass to them. The ball can be played at the first touch or controlled: in either case they must return it to the same player who made the pass.

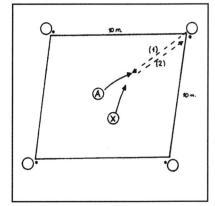

Objective: Receiving with opposition
Difficulty: 3
No. of players: Groups of 3
Material: One ball per group
Description: Player A passes the ball toward B, who must control in spite of the opposition of player X. Player X's function: he will try not only to block reception and get the ball but also will attempt to anticipate it.

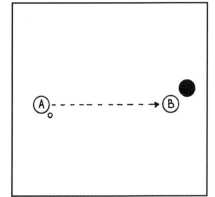

Objective: Receiving with opposition
Difficulty: 3
No. of players: Groups of 3
Material: One ball per group
Description: Player A passes the ball forward and players B and C, who are lined up with player A, vie for possession. Gradually increase the distance of the pass.

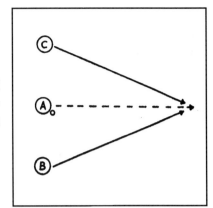

Objective: Receiving with opposition
Difficulty: 3
No. of players: Groups of 3
Material: One ball per group
Description: Player A passes the ball forward and players B and C, who are located some yards in front with their backs to A, vie for possession. Gradually increase the distance of the pass.

Objective: Receiving with opposition
Difficulty: 3
No. of players: Various groups
Material: One ball per group
Description: Player B receives different kinds of passes from player A. The players located outside the circle try to make player B's reception of the ball as difficult as possible but cannot enter the circle.

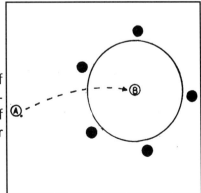

Objective: Receiving with opposition
Difficulty: 3
No. of players: Various groups
Material: 2-3 ball per group
Description: Player A sends the ball so that players B and C, located some 10 yards away, fight to get the ball. The player who gets possession of the ball gets one point for his team.

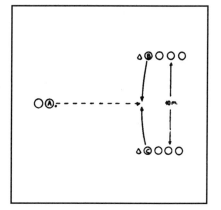

Objective: Receiving with opposition
Difficulty: 3
No. of players: Various groups
Material: 2 balls and 3 cones per group
Description: Player B begins a breaking away move toward cone 1 to receive teammate A's pass. Defender C attempts to intercept or disturb player B's reception, but only after the ball leaves player A's feet.

Directed control

Objective: Receiving - Directed control
Difficulty: 3
No. of players: One
Material: One ball per player
Description: Directed control with the inside of the foot: players throw the ball in the air and with only one contact bring the ball under control.

Objective: Receiving - Directed control
Difficulty: 3
No. of players: One
Material: One ball per player
Description: Directed control with outside of the foot: players throw the ball in the air and with only one contact bring the ball under control.

Objective: Receiving - Directed control
Difficulty: 3
No. of players: Groups of 2
Material: One ball per player
Description: Directed control with the chest: player A throws the ball in the air to player B, who receives it with the chest and with a turn of the trunk directs it to the side and down for rapid control.

Objective: Receiving - Directed control
Difficulty: 3
No. of players: Groups of 2
Material: One ball per player
Description: Directed control with the outside of the foot: player A passes the ball to B who receives with the outside of the foot, directing the ball with the first contact towards the opposite foot and returns the ball to A who does the same.

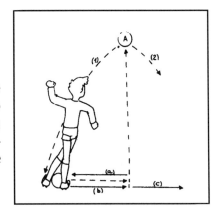

Objective: Receiving - Directed control
Difficulty: 3
No. of players: One
Material: One ball per player
Description: The players throw the ball into the air, when it falls they make a directed control with the inside of the foot, sending the ball behind the support leg.

Objective: Receiving - Directed control
Difficulty: 3
No. of players: One
Material: One ball per player
Description: Directed control with the heel: players throw the ball in the air; when it falls, they control with the heel, taking the ball from behind toward the front over the head.

Objective: Receiving - Directed control
Difficulty: 3
No. of players: Groups of 3
Material: One ball and one cone per group
Description: Player A sends the ball to B so that B, with directed control made with any part of the body, can "beat" the cone and return the ball to teammate A.

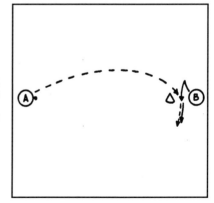

Objective: Receiving - Directed control
Difficulty: 3
No. of players: Groups of 2
Material: One ball and two cones per group
Description: The players must cover the distance between the cones by means of directed control. Player A sends the ball to B so that B, with directed control made with any part of the body, moves to the next cone and returns the ball to A.

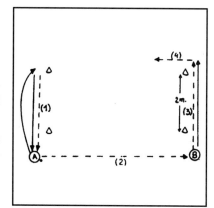

Objective: Receiving - Directed control
Difficulty: 3
No. of players: Groups of 2
Material: One ball and two cones per group
Description: Similar to the preceding exercise, but the passes are made diagonally.

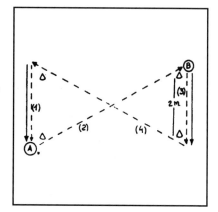

Objective: Receiving - Directed control
Difficulty: 3
No. of players: Groups of 3
Material: One ball per group
Description: Player B receives passes from A and C. On each reception, he makes directed controls to the inside, turns and passes to the other player who returns the pass on the opposite side. The passes of A and C should be first touch passes.

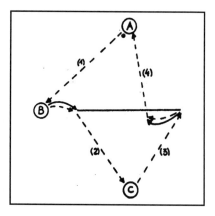

Objective: Receiving - Directed control
Difficulty: 3
No. of players: Groups of 3
Material: One ball per group
Description: Directed control while running: player A passes the ball to teammate B who runs to get it. When he gets to the ball he directs it to remain ready to pass to player C, and C begins the exercise again on the opposite side.

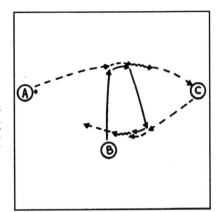

Objective: Receiving - Directed control
Difficulty: 3
No. of players: Groups of 4
Material: two balls per group
Description: Players A and B send passes to players C and D who make directed control to remain ready to pass to the players who are located behind their backs.

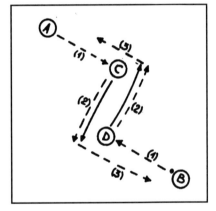

Application Plays

Objective: Receiving - Application plays
Difficulty: 3
No. of players: Various groups
Material: One ball per group
Description: Three players on either side of the neutral zone try to pass the ball among themselves but face two defenders who attempt to disrupt the passes as well as the receptions of the ball; no player can enter the neutral zone.

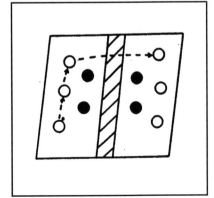

Objective: Receiving - Application plays
Difficulty: 3
No. of players: Various groups
Material: 4 balls per group
Description: Player's positions are shown in the diagram; the inside players are stationary while outside players move around the perimeter. The inside players pass the ball with different trajectories so that their teammates can make different kinds of receptions.

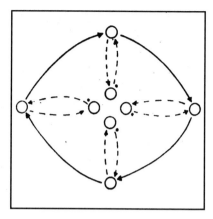

Objective: Reception - Application plays
Difficulty: 3
No. of players: Groups of 2
Material: 4 balls per group
Description: Players A and B attempt to cross their rival's end line; they may not use their hands.

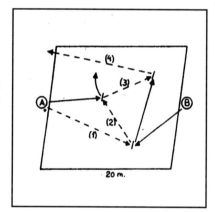

Objective: Receiving - Application plays
Difficulty: 3
No. of players: Groups of 4
Material: One ball per group
Description: Player A passes a long lobbed ball to teammate B; player B must get the ball in spite of the opposition of the two defenders who start 10 yards away and come out when A throws the ball.

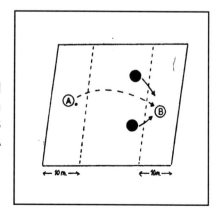

Objective: Receiving - Application plays
Difficulty: 3
No. of players: Groups of 4
Material: One ball per group
Description: This exercise is similar to the previous one. There are two possible receivers: A-B and C-D, who must receive the pass and at the same time play the ball among themselves to be able to make a second return pass. There are two defenders on each side to prevent receiving and to prevent the pass.

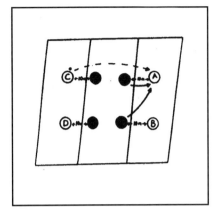

Objective: Receiving - Application plays
Difficulty: 3
No. of players: Groups of 4
Material: 3 balls per group
Description: Players B, C and D pass balls to their teammate A so that A, without knowing where they are going to pass the ball, tries to receive them; each possession of the ball means one point. They exchange positions so that all players play the receiver role.

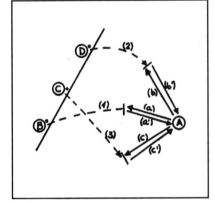

Objective: Receiving - Application plays
Difficulty: 3
No. of players: Various groups
Material: 6-8 balls per group
Description: The diagram indicates the position of the players; at the coach's signal the outside players pass balls for the inside player to control. Each controlled ball scores one point.

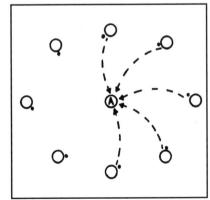

Objective: Receiving - Application plays
Difficulty: 3
No. of players: Various groups
Material: 3 balls per group
Description: The players are handless goalies, since they must receive the balls that are hit to them with any part of the body except the hands; once they have the ball they try to score in the opposing goal.

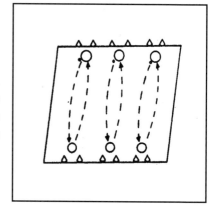

Objective: Receiving - Application plays
Difficulty: 3
No. of players: Various groups
Material: 5-6 balls per group
Description: Player X attempts to send the ball to his team who is on the outside of the play zone, the defending players try to prevent the ball from arriving at its destination. A point is earned for each ball that gets through.

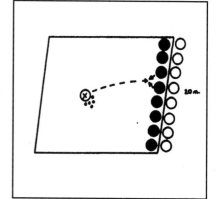

Objective: Receiving - Application plays
Difficulty: 3
No. of players: Various groups
Material: 5-6 balls per group
Description: Player P throws from his goalmouth; team Y occupying all the possible space, tries to prevent the ball from touching the ground. If they are successful, they attack the goal against two defenders.

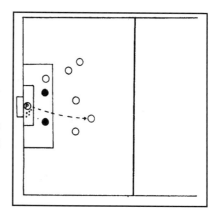

CHAPTER 5

TURNING AND FEINTING
Exercises for movement mechanics

Objective: Turning and Feinting: movement mechanics
Difficulty: 2
No. of players: One
Material: One ball per player and several cones
Description: The players dribble the ball and at each cone step on the ball and continue with a change of pace and/or direction to the next cone.

Objective: Turning and Feinting: movement mechanics
Difficulty: 3
No. of players: One
Material: One ball per player and several cones
Description: The player dribbles around a triangle formed by three cones. At each cone, he steps on the ball, pulls it back with the sole of his foot, turns and dribbles to the next cone.

Objective: Turning and Feinting: movement mechanics
Difficulty: 3
No. of players: Groups of 2
Material: One ball per player
Description: The same exercise of stopping the ball with the sole of the foot and retreating to get the ball back again rapidly in another direction in front of a defender who takes either a passive or active role.

Objective: Turning and Feinting: movement mechanics
Difficulty: 3
No. of players: One
Material: One ball per player and several cones
Description: Coming out with the inside of the foot; the players dribble the ball toward the cone and when they arrive in front of it, they make a change of direction with the inside of the foot.

Objective: Turning and Feinting: movement mechanics
Difficulty: 3
No. of players: One
Material: One ball per player and several cones
Description: The players cover the distance along a line of cones and at each one they make the change of direction with the inside of the foot.

Objective: Turning and Feinting: movement mechanics
Difficulty: 3
No. of players: Groups of 2
Material: One ball per player
Description: The player dribbles the ball toward the defender to make a change of direction in front of him with the inside of the foot.

Objective: Turning and Feinting: movement mechanics
Difficulty: 3
No. of players: One
Material: One ball per player and several cones
Description: Change of direction with the outside of the foot; the players dribble the ball and in front of each cone make a change of direction with the outside of the foot.

Objective: Turning and Feinting: movement mechanics
Difficulty: 3
No. of players: One
Material: One ball per player and several cones
Description: The players run a course divided into different zones; in each one of the zones, they must change direction with the outside of the foot.

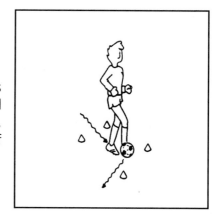

Objective: Turning and Feinting: movement mechanics
Difficulty: 3
No. of players: One
Material: One ball per player
Description: Players dribble the ball toward a defender and make a change of direction with the outside of the foot.

Objective: Turning and Feinting: movement mechanics
Difficulty: 3
No. of players: One
Material: One ball per player and several cones
Description: Double inside – inside contact. The players dribble the ball and in front of each cone they make contact with the inside of the foot to unbalance the opponent and rapidly make the second contact with the inside of the opposite foot.

Objective: Turning and Feinting: movement mechanics
Difficulty: 3
No. of players: One
Material: One ball per player and several cones
Description: Players run on a divided course in different zones; in each one they must make the previous dribble (inside-inside).

Objective: Turning and Feinting: movement mechanics
Difficulty: 3
No. of players: One
Material: One ball per player
Description: Players dribble the ball toward the defender and make an inside-inside dribble in front of him.

Objective: Turning and Feinting: movement mechanics
Difficulty: 3
No. of players: One
Material: One ball per player and several cones
Description: Double contact inside-outside: the players dribble the ball and in front of each cone they make contact with the inside of the foot to unbalance the opponent and make the second contact with the outside to get by him on the opposite side.

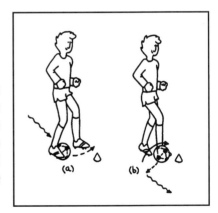

Objective: Turning and Feinting: movement mechanics
Difficulty: 3
No. of players: One
Material: One ball per player and several cones
Description: The players run a course divided in different zones; in each one they must make the previous dribble (inside-outside).

Objective: Turning and Feinting: movement mechanics
Difficulty: 3
No. of players: One
Material: One ball per player
Description: The players dribble the ball toward the defender and make an inside-outside dribble in front of him.

Objective: Turning and Feinting: movement mechanics
Difficulty: 3
No. of players: One
Material: One ball per player and several cones
Description: The tunnel or little bridge: the players dribble the ball and in front of the two cones pass the ball between the cones and rapidly regain possession of the ball.

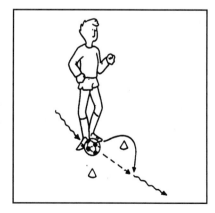

Objective: Turning and Feinting: movement mechanics
Difficulty: 3
No. of players: One
Material: One ball per player
Description: The players dribble the ball toward the defender and send it between his legs (nutmeg) to regain control on the other side.

Objective: Turning and Feinting: movement mechanics
Difficulty: 3
No. of players: One
Material: One ball per player and several cones
Description: Bypass: the players dribble the ball and in front of the cone push the ball by one side while running around the other side to regain control.

Objective: Turning and Feinting: movement mechanics
Difficulty: 3
No. of players: One
Material: One ball per player
Description: The players dribble the ball toward the defender and push it to one side as in the previous exercise.

Objective: Turning and Feinting: movement mechanics
Difficulty: 4
No. of players: Various groups
Material: 4-5 balls per group
Description: Player A passes the ball to B and follows his pass to defend; when B gets it, he gets by A by either pushing it by or through his legs, passes to C and follows his pass to defend and so on.

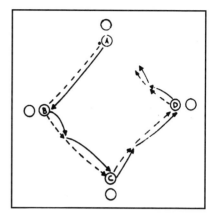

Objective: Turning and Feinting: movement mechanics
Difficulty: 4
No. of players: One
Material: One ball per player and several cones
Description: The box: players drive the ball toward the cone; when they get to the cone they make a contact with the inside of the foot farthest from the cone passing the ball behind the support leg and changing direction.

Objective: Turning and Feinting: movement mechanics
Difficulty: 4
No. of players: One
Material: One ball per player and several cones
Description: Players run a course divided into different zones, in each one they must make the dribble described in the previous exercise.

Objective: Turning and Feinting: movement mechanics
Difficulty: 4
No. of players: One
Material: One ball per player and several cones
Description: Players run a square course as the diagram indicates, making the changes of direction as in the previous exercise.

Objective: Turning and Feinting: movement mechanics
Difficulty: 4
No. of players: One
Material: One ball per player
Description: The players dribble the ball toward the defenders and get by them using the technique described in the previous exercise.

Objective: Turning and Feinting: movement mechanics
Difficulty: 4
No. of players: Groups of 4
Material: One ball per player and 4 cones
Description: Players A and B dribble toward the cone and the defenders block their way; when this happens they make box dribbles to return again to the next cone where the second defender blocks their way, etc.

Objective: Turning and Feinting: movement mechanics
Difficulty: 4
No. of players: One
Material: One ball per player
Description: Double feint. The player pretends to go to one side and goes to the other using the inside of the foot. The player dribbles the ball toward the cone; when he gets up to the cone, he double feints (spars) with his body toward the left and the right to come out rapidly with the inside of his left leg.

Objective: Turning and Feinting: movement mechanics
Difficulty: 4
No. of players: One
Material: One ball per player and several cones
Description: The players run a course divided in different zones; in each one they must dribble as described in the previous exercise.

Objective: Turning and Feinting: movement mechanics
Difficulty: 4
No. of players: One
Material: One ball per player
Description: The players dribble the ball toward the defenders and get by them using the technique described in the previous exercise.

Objective: Turning and Feinting: movement mechanics
Difficulty: 4
No. of players: One
Material: One ball per player and several cones
Description: Double feint, coming out with the outside of the foot. The player dribbles the ball toward the cone; at the cone he makes a double feint with his body toward the left and the right to come out rapidly with the outside of the right leg.

Objective: Turning and Feinting: movement mechanics
Difficulty: 4
No. of players: One
Material: One ball per player and several cones
Description: The players run a course divided in different zones; in each one they must use the technique described in the previous exercise.

Objective: Turning and Feinting: movement mechanics
Difficulty: 4
No. of players: One
Material: One ball per player
Description: The players dribble the ball toward the defenders and get by them using the technique described in the previous exercise.

Objective: Turning and Feinting: movement mechanics
Difficulty: 4
No. of players: One
Material: One ball per player and several cones
Description: Pass the leg over the ball and come out with the outside of the foot. The player dribbles the ball toward the cone; at the cone he takes the dribbling foot to the opposite side of the ball and with the outside of the same foot pushes the ball in the other direction.

Objective: Turning and Feinting: movement mechanics
Difficulty: 4
No. of players: One
Material: One ball per player and several cones
Description: The players run a course divided into different zones; in each one they must use the technique described in the previous exercise.

Objective: Turning and Feinting: movement mechanics
Difficulty: 4
No. of players: One
Material: One ball per player
Description: The players drive the ball toward the defenders and get by them using the technique described in the previous exercise.

Objective: Turning and Feinting: movement mechanics
Difficulty: 4
No. of players: One
Material: One ball per player and several cones
Description: The bicycle: the player dribbles the ball toward the cone; at the cone, he moves one leg in front of the ball as if in preparation for a heel pass, then pulls the leg back over the ball and pushes it forward with the same foot to continue dribbling.

Objective: Turning and Feinting: movement mechanics
Difficulty: 4
No. of players: One
Material: One ball per player and several cones
Description: The players run a course divided into different zones; in each one, they must make the dribble described in the previous exercise.

Objective: Turning and Feinting: movement mechanics
Difficulty: 4
No. of players: One
Material: One ball per player
Description: The players dribble the ball toward the defenders and get by them using the dribble described in the previous exercise.

Objective: Turning and Feinting: movement mechanics
Difficulty: 4
No. of players: One
Material: One ball per player and several cones
Description: Pass the leg over the ball and come out with the outside of the other foot: the player dribbles the ball toward the cones; at the cone, he crosses the dribbling leg over the ball to freeze the defender and moves in the opposite direction using the outside of the trailing foot.

Objective: Turning and Feinting: movement mechanics
Difficulty: 4
No. of players: One
Material: One ball per player and several cones
Description: The player make a run as indicated in the diagram, dribbling as described in the previous exercises.

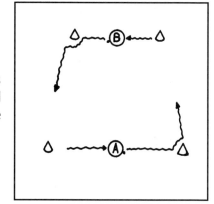

Objective: Turning and Feinting: movement mechanics
Difficulty: 4
No. of players: One
Material: One ball per player
Description: The players dribble the ball toward the defenders and get by them using the dribble described in the previous exercise.

Objective: Turning and Feinting: movement mechanics
Difficulty: 4
No. of players: One
Material: One ball per player and several cones
Description: The players run a course divided into different zones; in each one they must dribble as described in the previous exercise.

Objective: Turning and Feinting: movement mechanics
Difficulty: 4
No. of players: One
Material: One ball per player and several cones
Description: Players make a run, such as indicated in the graph, dribbling as described in the previous exercises.

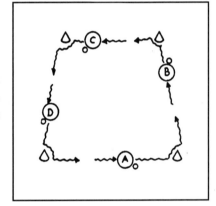

Objective: Turning and Feinting: movement mechanics
Difficulty: 4
No. of players: One
Material: One ball per player and two cones
Description: Player A makes a pass to X who returns it to him and comes out to meet him; A must get by him, circle the cone and move toward the other player X to repeat the same exercise.

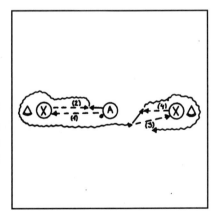

Objective: Turning and Feinting: movement mechanics
Difficulty: 4
No. of players: One
Material: One ball per player
Description: Player A dribbles the ball and faces a line of opponents who run toward him; he has to get by them with the dribble established by the coach.

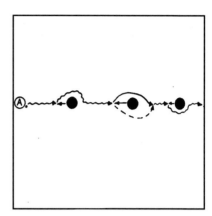

Objective: Turning and Feinting: movement mechanics
Difficulty: 4
No. of players: Various groups
Material: One ball per player
Description: Player A dribbles the ball and faces a line of opponents who run toward him; he has to get by each defender with a different dribble.

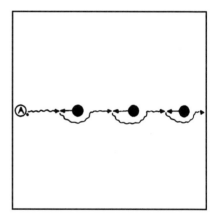

Objective: Turning and Feinting: movement mechanics
Difficulty: 4
No. of players: One
Material: One ball per player and several cones
Description: Player A dribbles the ball through a narrow passageway, with some hoops located randomly to the right and to the left; each time player A comes upon a cone he must rapidly place his leg in the inside of the hoop and begin dribbling the ball again.

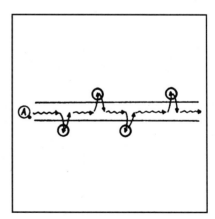

Objective: Turning and Feinting: movement mechanics
Difficulty: 4
No. of players: One
Material: One ball per player and several cones
Description: Player A dribbles differently at each cone; when he arrives at the last cone, he must pass the ball to B who repeats the same movement.

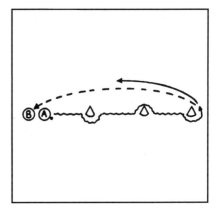

Exercises in 1 v 1 situations

Objective: 1 v 1 exercises
Difficulty: 2
No. of players: Groups of 2
Material: One ball and 4 cones per group
Description: Player X attempts to get by his opponent Y and pass through the goalmouth; each time he succeeds, he earns a point. Roles are reversed when the defender gets the ball away from the opponent.

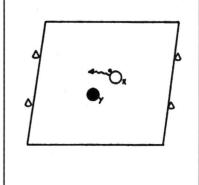

Objective: 1 v 1 exercises
Difficulty: 2
No. of players: Various groups
Material: 3 balls and 12 cones per group
Description: Exercise similar to the previous one, but in this case the defending players, if they are from the same team, can help each other by entering into the adjacent field.

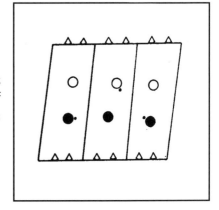

Objective: 1 v 1 exercises
Difficulty: 3
No. of players: Groups of 2
Material: One ball and 8 cones per group
Description: X v Y; each one of them defends two goals and attacks two goalmouths. Player X defends goalmouths 1 and 2, while player Y defends goalmouths 3 and 4.

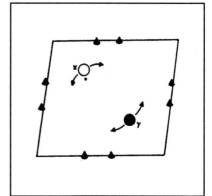

Objective: 1 v 1 exercises
Difficulty: 3
No. of players: Various groups
Material: 4 balls and 8 cones per group
Description: Each pair can attack any goal. To score a point they have to dribble through the cones.

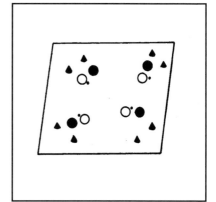

Objective: 1 x 1 exercises
Difficulty: 3
No. of players: Groups of 2
Material: One ball and two cones per group
Description: Player A must try to get by player X and dribble between the cones.

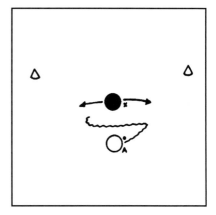

Objective: 1 v 1 exercises
Difficulty: 3
No. of players: Groups of 4
Material: Two balls per group
Description: Players A and B attempt to enter the area defended by the X players.

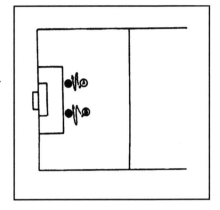

Objective: 1 v 1 exercises
Difficulty: 3
No. of players: Groups of 4
Material: Two balls per group
Description: Players A and B must try to get to the penalty line; players X try to prevent it and at the same time regain possession of the ball. If they get the ball they try to dribble to the goal line. Each time the team gets to the goal line they win a point.

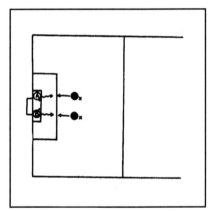

Objective: 1 v 1 exercises
Difficulty: 3
No. of players: Various groups
Material: 4-5 balls per group
Description: Player A tries to dribble to all the defenders who occupy their determined zones; they can't help each other.

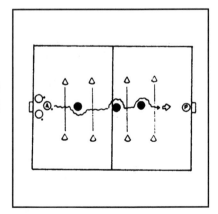

Objective: 1 v 1 exercises
Difficulty: 3
No. of players: Various groups
Material: One ball per group
Description: Player A passes the ball to C and comes out to meet him. C tries to beat A's opposition and if he succeeds, he passes to B and the exercise is repeated.

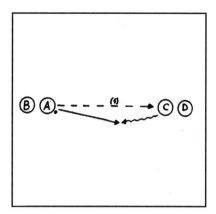

Objective: 1 x 1 exercises
Difficulty: 3
No. of players: Groups of 3
Material: One ball per group
Description: Player P throws the ball so that players A and B fight for it. The player that gets the ball becomes an offensive player and tries to beat his teammate's opposition and invade P's goalmouth.

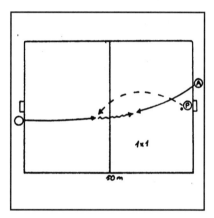

Objective: 1 v 1 exercises
Difficulty: 3
No. of players: Groups of 3
Material: One ball per player
Description: Player P throws the ball so that players A and B fight for it. The player that gets the ball becomes an offensive player and tries to beat his teammate's opposition and invade P's goalmouth.

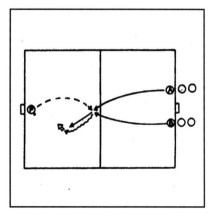

Objective: 1 v 1 exercises
Difficulty: 3
No. of players: Groups of 3
Material: One ball per group
Description: Player P throws the ball low so that players A and B fight for it. The player that gets the ball becomes an offensive player and tries to beat his teammate's opposition and invade P's goalmouth.

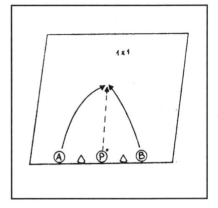

Objective: 1 v 1 exercises
Difficulty: 3
No. of players: Groups of 3
Material: One ball and 6 cones per group
Description: Player P throws the ball low so that players A and B fight for it. The player that gets the ball becomes an offensive player. Each player defends the goalmouth that is at his back. If the offensive player passes the ball through his teammate's goal, he scores one point. If he manages to dribble through P's goal, he scores two points.

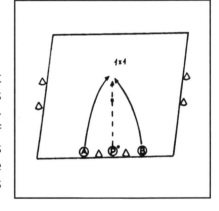

Objective: 1 v 1 exercises
Difficulty: 3
No. of players: Various groups
Material: One ball per group
Description: Players X and Y fight among themselves for possession of the ball. To keep it, they can use the support players who are located at the corners of the play area and will always return the ball first time to the one who passed it to them.

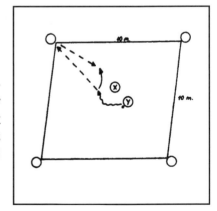

Objective: 1 v 1 exercises
Difficulty: 3
No. of players: Various groups
Material: One ball per group
Description: Players X and Y fight between themselves to get the ball. To keep it they can use their own team's support players who are located at the corners of the play area and will return it to them with a first time pass.

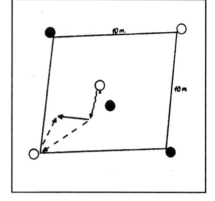

Objective: 1 v 1 exercises
Difficulty: 3
No. of players: Various groups
Material: Two balls per group
Description: Each player in possession of the ball has 30 seconds to keep it; at the end of this time a replacement player takes his place.

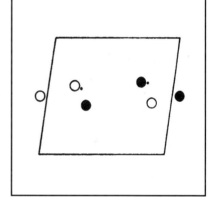

Objective: 1 v 1 exercises
Difficulty: 3
No. of players: Various groups
Material: Two balls per group
Description: The player who is in possession of the ball must dribble past his opponent and rapidly make a pass to a teammate located along the sides of the playing area. If there is no dribble-pass or if they are dispossessed by the defender, the roles are reversed.

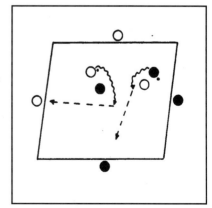

Objective: 1 v 1 exercises
Difficulty: 3
No. of players: Groups of 4
Material: One ball per group
Description: Player X must try to beat his defender and at the same time attempt to get a pass to his teammate who is in the opposite field.

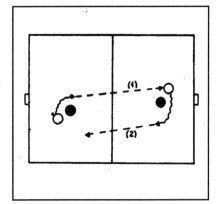

Objective: 1 v 1 exercises
Difficulty: 3
No. of players: Groups of 4
Material: One ball per group
Description: Player A passes the ball to B and breaks away right or left to receive a return pass; once he receives the pass he must beat defender X and try to invade P's goalmouth.

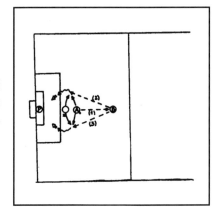

Objective: 1 v 1 exercises
Difficulty: 3
No. of players: Various groups
Material: One ball per group
Description: Player A passes the ball to B so that he can beat defender X and invade P's goalmouth.

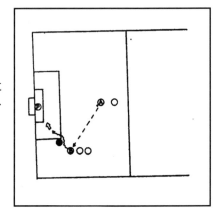

Objective: 1 v 1 exercises
Difficulty: 4
No. of players: Various groups
Material: One ball per group
Description: Play of passes between players A and B so that B begins breaking away and receives teammate A's pass; once he receives the pass he tries to beat defender X.

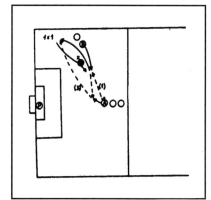

Objective: 1 v 1 exercises
Difficulty: 4
No. of players: Various groups
Material: One ball per group
Description: Play of passes among players A, B, and C so that A begins breaking away and receives the pass from teammate B; once he receives the pass he attempts to beat the defender X and invade P's goalmouth.

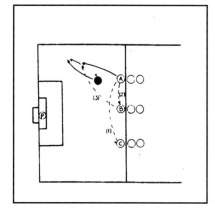

Objective: 1 v 1 exercises
Difficulty: 4
No. of players: Various groups
Material: One ball per group
Description: Player A sends a pass to teammate B who may choose between A and C to make a pass to (both players make a break away movement); the player who receives attempts to beat defender X and invade P's goalmouth.

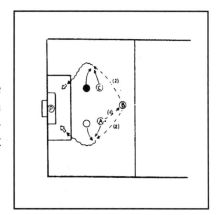

Objective: 1 v 1 exercise
Difficulty: 4
No. of players: Various groups
Material: One ball per group
Description: Player A sends a pass to his team-mate B, who may choose among A, C, and D to make a pass to; the player who receives tries to beat defender X and invade P's goalmouth.

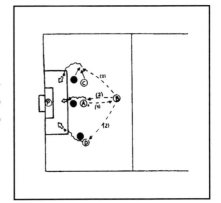

Objective: 1 v 1 exercise
Difficulty: 4
No. of players: Various groups
Material: One ball per group
Description: Player P throws the ball so that players X and Y fight over it, and the player who gets it attempts to invade the opposing goalmouth. At the same time the same exercise is developed on the opposite side

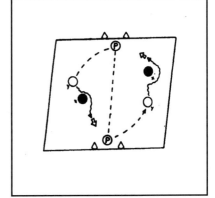

Objective: 1 v 1 exercise
Difficulty: 4
No. of players: Various groups
Material: Two balls per group
Description: Player A tosses the ball to B who with his head passes it to C. C begins dribbling and must get by B who is running toward the center to receive the pass from E who previously received from D.

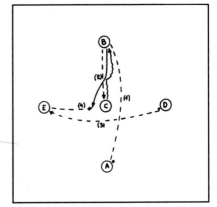

Objective: 1 v 1 exercise
Difficulty: 2
No. of players: Groups of 2
Material: One ball per group
Description: The player who dribbles the ball must beat the defender who is 5 yards away. The defending player is seated and has to get up to avoid being beaten; he can't get up until the opponent starts running.

Objective: 1 v 1 exercise
Difficulty: 2
No. of players: Groups of 2
Material: One ball per group
Description: The player who dribbles the ball must beat the defender who is 5 yards away. The defensive player is lying down and has to get up to avoid being beaten; he can't get up until the opponent starts running.

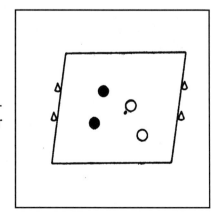

Exercises in numerical equality situations

Objective: Dribbling: numerical equality exercises
Difficulty: 3
No. of players: Groups of 4
Material: One ball and 4 cones per group
Description: 2 v 2 to try to score in the opponent's goal; in order to score a goal, a player must have beaten his opponent with a dribble.

Objective: Dribbling: numerical equality exercises
Difficulty: 1
No. of players: Groups of 4
Material: One ball per group
Description: 2 v 2 + 1 goalie to score in the opponent's goal; in order to score a goal, a player must have beaten his opponent with a dribble.

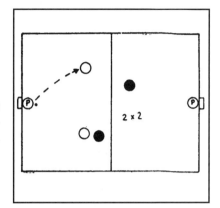

Objective: Dribbling: numerical equality exercises
Difficulty: 3
No. of players: Groups of 4
Material: One ball and 8 cones per group
Description: 2 v 2 to try to score in the opponent's goal; in order to score a goal, a player must have beaten his opponent with a dribble. Team X attacks goals 3 and 4, and team Y goals 1 and 2.

Objective: Dribbling: numerical equality exercises
Difficulty: 3
No. of players: Various groups
Material: One ball
Description: The players are positioned in four zones as the diagram indicates. The first player Y must enter X's zone, beat him and make a pass to his teammate in the second zone unless he can cross the line that marks the first zone. The second player Y, when he receives the ball, repeats the same exercise.

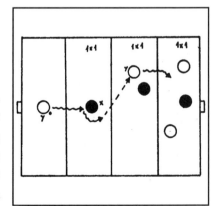

Objective: Dribbling: numerical equality exercises
Difficulty: 3
No. of players: Various groups
Material: One ball and 4 cones per group
Description: The players are distributed in three different zones as the diagram indicates. The players try to beat their defenders and pass the ball to their teammate in the 2nd zone, who when he receives attempts to pass to his teammates in the 3rd zone. No player can cross the boundary lines.

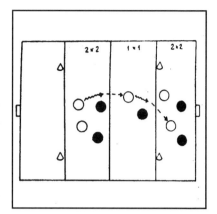

Objective: Dribbling: numerical equality exercises
Difficulty: 3
No. of players: Various groups
Material: One ball and 4 cones per group
Description: The players are distributed in three zones as the diagram indicates. The players play together to overcome their defenders and dribble into the 2nd zone. The player who does so plays with his teammate in that zone to attempt to dribble into the 3rd zone. The player who does that plays with two teammates in a 3 v 2 to score.

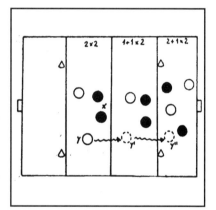

Objective: Dribbling: numerical equality exercises
Difficulty: 3
No. of players: Various groups
Material: One ball and 4 cones per group
Description: The players are distributed in three zones as the diagram indicates. The players play among themselves to beat their defenders and pass to their teammates in the 2nd zone, who then try to pass to the 3rd zone. We highlight the necessity of dribbling before passing.

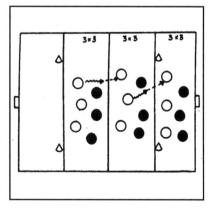

Objective: Dribbling: numerical equality exercises
Difficulty: 4
No. of players: Various groups
Material: One ball per group
Description: Players are distributed in three zones as the diagram indicates. The players play among themselves to try to beat their defenders and dribble into the 2nd zone; the player who does that plays with his teammates to move into the 3rd zone; the player who does that plays with his teammates to cross the end line.

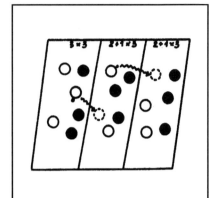

Objective: Dribbling: numerical equality exercises
Difficulty: 4
No. of players: Various groups
Material: One ball and 4 cones per group
Description: Players are distributed in three zones as the diagram indicates. The players play among themselves to try to beat their defenders and dribble into the 2nd zone; the player who does that plays with his teammates to dribble into the 3rd zone; the player who does that plus one other play with their teammates in a 4 v 4 to beat the defenders.

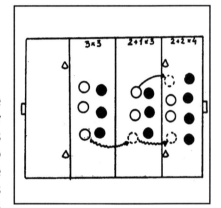

Objective: Dribbling: numerical equality exercises
Difficulty: 4
No. of players: Various groups
Material: One ball and 4 cones per group
Description: Players are distributed in three zones as the diagram indicates. Player Y must get by X to pass the ball to his 2nd zone teammates, who in their turn, must do the same against their defenders to pass the ball to their 3rd zone teammates who try to score.

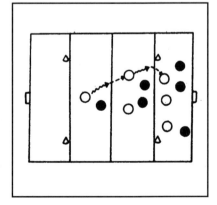

Exercises in numerical inferiority situations

Objective: Dribbling: numerical inferiority exercises
Difficulty: 3
No. of players: Various groups
Material: One ball and 4 cones per group
Description: The players are located in three zones as the diagram indicates. Player Y must get by the X defenders to pass the ball to his 2nd zone teammate, who must beat his defender to pass the ball to his 3rd zone teammates who in turn try to score.

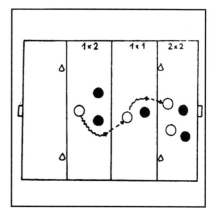

Objective: Dribbling: numerical inferiority exercises
Difficulty: 3
No. of players: Various groups
Material: One ball and 4 cones per group
Description: Players are located in three zones as the diagram indicates. In all the zones one attacker plays against two defenders; before a pass can be made to the next zone, the player must beat one defender with a dribble.

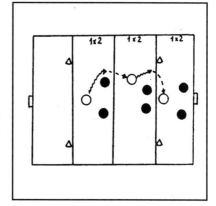

Objective: Dribbling: numerical inferiority exercises
Difficulty: 3
No. of players: Various groups
Material: One ball and 4 cones per group
Description: 2 v 3 to attack the goal. The free player always plays with the defending team.

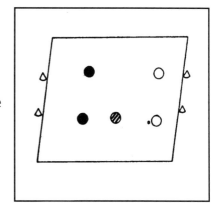

Objective: Dribbling: numerical inferiority exercises
Difficulty: 3
No. of players: Various groups
Material: One ball per group
Description: 2 v 3. (Two offensive players confront three defensive players.) There is a free player who always plays as a defender. The attackers try to dribble and pass each other the ball; 5 passes scores 1 point. A pass cannot be made unless the player has first beaten one defender with the dribble.

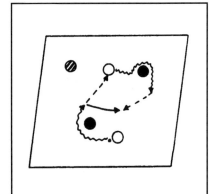

Objective: Dribbling: numerical inferiority exercises
Difficulty: 3
No. of players: Various groups
Material: One ball and 4 cones per group
Description: The players are distributed in three zones as the diagram indicates. The Y players must beat their defenders to pass the ball to their 2nd zone teammates who try to pass the ball to the 3rd zone.

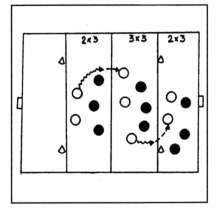

Objective: Dribbling: numerical inferiority exercises
Difficulty: 3
No. of players: Various groups
Material: One ball and 4 cones per group
Description: The players are distributed in three zones as the diagram indicates. The Y players must beat their defenders to pass the ball to their 2nd zone teammates who must do the same to pass the ball to the 3rd zone.

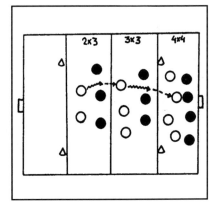

Objective: Dribbling: numerical inferiority
exercises
Difficulty: 4
No. of players: Various groups
Material: One ball and 4 cones per group
Description: 3 v 3 + 1 neutral player to score.
There is a free player who always plays with
the defending team.

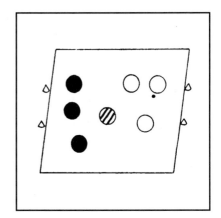

Objective: Dribbling: numerical inferiority
exercises
Difficulty: 4
No. of players: Various groups
Material: One ball and 4 cones
Description: The players are distributed in three
zones as the diagram indicates. The Y players
must beat their defenders to pass the ball to
their 2nd zone teammates who must do the
same to pass the ball to the 3rd zone.

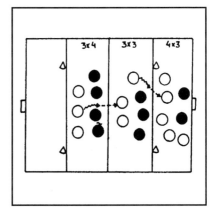

Objective: Dribbling: numerical inferiority
exercises
Difficulty: 4
No. of players: Various groups
Material: 4-5 ball and 2 cones per group
Description: Player A tries to dribble over the
broken line defended by player X. At the same
time, two X players come out running from the
zone corners to go to the aid of their defending
teammate X and prevent A from dribbling over
the line.

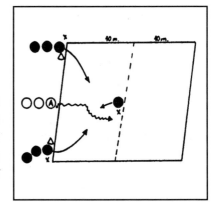

Objective: Dribbling: numerical inferiority exercises
Difficulty: 4
No. of players: Various groups
Material: 4-5 balls and 4 cones per group
Description: Player A tries to dribble over the broken line defended by player X. At the same time, two X players come out running from the zone corners to go to the aid of their defending teammate X and prevent A from dribbling over the line. If A makes it over the line he will begin again in the 2nd zone.

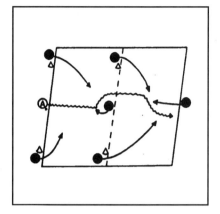

Application plays

Objective: Dribble: Application plays
Difficulty: 3
No. of players: Various groups
Material: 4-5 balls per group
Description: The Y players must dribble through three defensive zones guarded by three defenders, who may not help each other (each defends only his own zone).

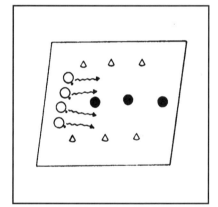

Objective: Dribble: Application plays
Difficulty: 3
No. of players: Various groups
Material: 4-5 balls per group
Description: Players A and B must attempt to pass over the defensive barrier consisting of three X players. If they do it, they may recover and prepare the new strategy, in the neutral zone, to attempt to break through the second barrier.

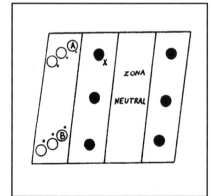

Objective: Dribble: Application plays
Difficulty: 3
No. of players: Various groups
Material: 4-5 balls
Description: Each pair defends its own cone; if one member of the pair manages to touch the opposing pairs cone with the ball, his team gets 1 point.

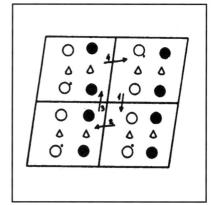

Objective: Dribble: Application plays
Difficulty: 3
No. of players: Various groups
Material: 3 balls per group
Description: Three simultaneous 1 v 1 matches to score in either goal. Each team gets 30 seconds to score as many goals possible, then the roles are switched.

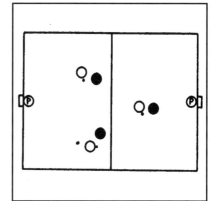

Objective: Dribble: Application plays
Difficulty: 3
No. of players: Various groups
Material: One ball per group
Description: 3 v 3 to take the ball into the corner zone of the opposite team which is defended by 1 player.

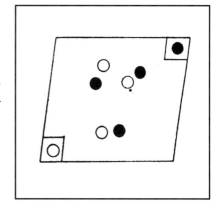

Objective: Dribble: Application plays
Difficulty: 3
No. of players: Various groups
Material: One ball and 12 cones per group
Description: 2 teams, each with the objective of scoring in the opposing goal with free touches. If a player dribbles through one of the small goals, the opposing team must allow him free passage, but he may not shoot on goal; he must pass to a teammate.

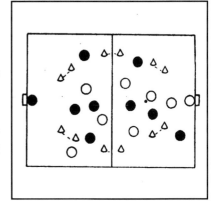

Objective: Dribble: Application plays
Difficulty: 3
No. of players: Various groups
Material: One ball per group
Description: Two teams with equal numbers play freely for ball possession. At the coach's signal, the player who has the ball must try to beat the nearest defender with the dribble. If he succeeds, he scores a point for his team; if he fails, possession goes to the other team and play continues.

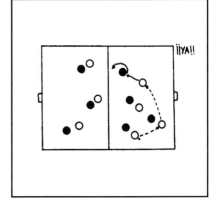

Objective: Dribble: Application plays
Difficulty: 3
No. of players: Various groups
Material: One ball per group
Description: Two teams with equal numbers play with the objective of scoring in the rival team's goal. In each half there are two corner zones where if an opponent receives the ball, only one defender can cut him off (no double-teaming in the corners).

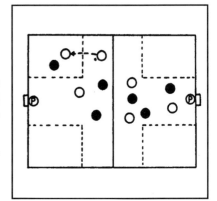

Objective: Dribble: Application plays
Difficulty: 3
No. of players: Various groups
Material: One ball per group
Description: The diagram indicates the position of the four teams. Each team's players play together to keep possession of the ball and when there is a possibility, one makes a pass to his teammates in the diagonal zone.

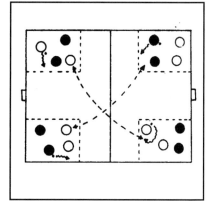

Objective: Dribble: Application plays
Difficulty: 3
No. of players: Various groups
Material: One ball per group
Description: The diagram indicates the position of the four teams. Each team's players play together to keep possession of the ball and when there is a possibility, one makes a pass to his teammates in the adjacent zone.

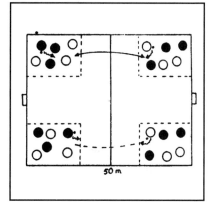

Objective: Dribble: Application plays
Difficulty: 3
No. of players: Various groups
Material: 3 balls per group
Description: The team in possession of the ball must try to get into the marked zones in the corners, and the defending team must prevent it. Each time they manage to enter scores a point.

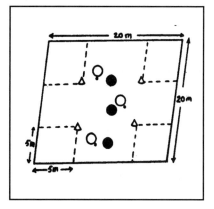

Objective: Dribble: Application plays
Difficulty: 3
No. of players: Various groups
Material: One ball per group
Description: Three players try to get through three defensive zones against the presence of the two defenders in each zone. The defenders may only defend in their own zone. When an offensive player passes the zones boundary, his teammates may also pass.

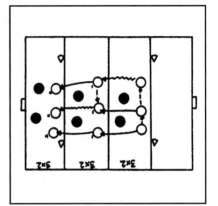

Objective: Dribble: Application plays
Difficulty: 3
No. of players: Various groups
Material: One ball and 4 cones per group
Description: The players of the two teams are located some 10 yards from the ball and each has a number. When the coach calls a number, the two players with that number come out after the ball and vie for possession. They then play 1 v 1 to score in the two small goals.

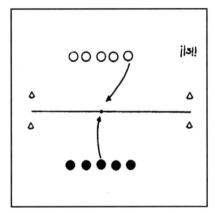

Objective: Dribble: Application plays
Difficulty: 3
No. of players: Various groups
Material: 7 balls per group
Description: All the players of one team have the ball within their own area. At the coach's signal they must cross the opponent's field where the players from the other team try to steal the greatest number of balls possible. Each player who makes it through with the ball scores a point for his team.

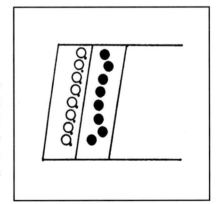

Chapter 6

SHOOTING
Exercises for movement mechanics

Objective: Shooting: movement mechanics
Difficulty: 2
No. of players: Groups of 6-8
Material: 3-4 and 10-12 cones per group
Description: Players are in threes with a goalie and a player on each side of the goal. They shoot on goal alternately. Shots are taken with a static ball and with different surface contacts.

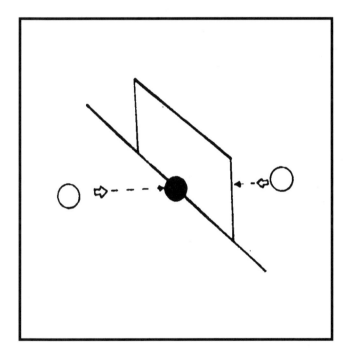

Objectives: Shooting: movement mechanics
Difficulty: 2
No. of players: Groups of 10-12
Material: 5-6 balls per group
Description: Players are divided into two groups and stand on either side of the goal. One group shoots while the other shags. After all balls have been shot, roles are reversed.

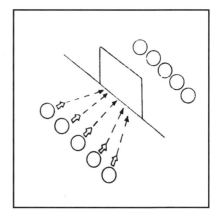

Objective: Shooting: movement mechanics
Difficulty: 2
No. of players: Groups of 5-6
Material: 5-6 balls and one cone per group
Description: Players stand along the 18 yard line, each with a ball. In turn, they run out around the cone, leaving their ball, and return to shoot on goal.

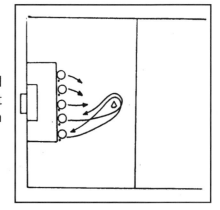

Objective: Shooting: movement mechanics
Difficulty: 2
No. of players: Groups of 5-6
Material: 5-6 balls and a cone per group
Description: The balls are located on the 18 yard line. Each player must shoot all the balls. After each shot, the player must circle the cone before taking the next shot.

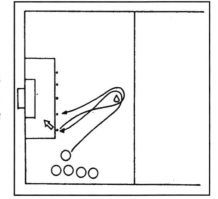

Objective: Shooting: movement mechanics
Difficulty: 3
No. of players: Groups of 5-6
Material: One ball per player
Description: The players are divided into two groups; some are located to the right of the goalmouth and the others to the left. Both groups shoot to the far post.

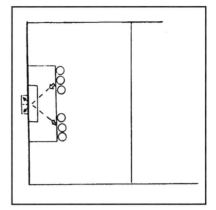

Objective: Shooting: movement mechanics
Difficulty: 3
No. of players: Groups of 5-6
Material: One ball per player
Description: The distribution of the players is similar to the previous exercise. In this case shots are directed at the near post.

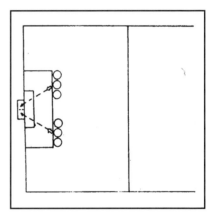

Objective: Shooting: movement mechanics
Difficulty: 4
No. of players: Groups of 6-8
Material: One ball per player and two hoops
Description: The players are divided into two groups: each player directs his toward one of the hoops hung from the goalmouth.

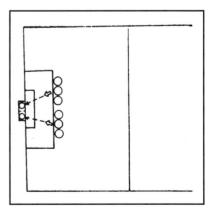

Objective: Shooting: movement mechanics
Difficulty: 4
No. of players: Groups of 5-6
Material: One ball per player
Description: Two groups of players are located in the corners of the penalty area. Shots must pass inside the cones placed on the corners of the 6 yard box.

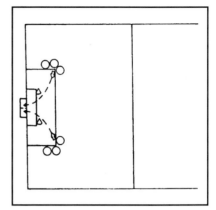

Objective: Shooting: movement mechanics
Difficulty: 4
No. of players: Groups of 2-4
Material: One ball per pair
Description: Each player defends his goal and attacks the opposition. The player who defends is located 3-4 yards from the goalmouth. The shooter tries to loft the shot over the defender and into the goal.

Objective: Shooting: movement mechanics
Difficulty: 3
No. of players: Groups of 5-6
Material: One ball per player
Description: Two groups of players and two goals positioned as the diagram indicates. The players direct their shots toward the farthest goal.

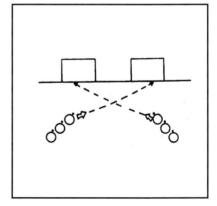

Objective: Shooting: movement mechanics
Difficulty: 3
No. of players: Groups of 2
Material: One ball and 4 cones per group
Description: Players X and Y, each positioned in his own goalmouth exchange shots. The shots can be made with different contact surfaces.

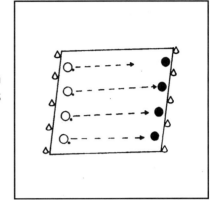

Objective: Shooting: movement mechanics
Difficulty: 3
No. of players: Groups of 4-5
Material: 5 balls and 5 cones per group
Description: Player A must pass by each cone and shoot on goal.

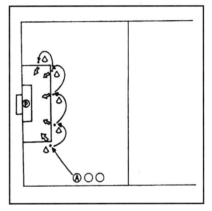

Objective: Shooting: movement mechanics
Difficulty: 3
No. of players: Groups of 4-5
Material: 5 balls
Description: Player A must shoot to the goal defended by player P and the 3-man wall. He can shoot around or over the wall.

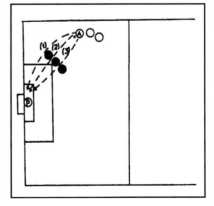

Objective: Shooting: movement mechanics
Difficulty: 3
No. of players: Groups of 4-5
Material: 4-5 balls per group
Description: Exercise similar to the previous one, but now the shot is taken from in front.

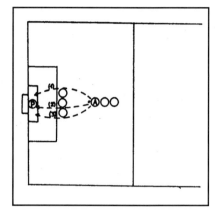

Objective: Shooting: movement mechanics
Difficulty: 3
No. of players: Various groups
Material: One ball per player
Description: Players are located in different positions all along the edge of the penalty area; they must shoot to the goal defended by player P, following the established order.

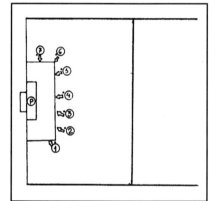

Objective: Shooting: movement mechanics
Difficulty: 3
No. of players: Various groups
Material: One ball per player
Description: Exercise similar to the previous one. In this case the coach shouts a number and the corresponding player shoots to the goal defended by player P.

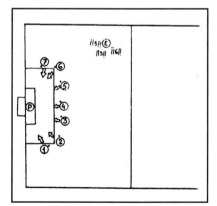

Shooting after a forward pass

Objective: Shooting: after a forward pass
Difficulty: 2
No. of players: Various groups
Material: 4-5 balls per group
Description: Player A sends a pass to his teammate B who returns the ball to him on the right or left so that A shoots to the goal defended by player C.

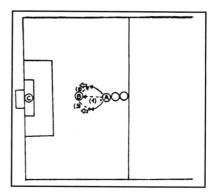

Objective: Shooting: after a forward pass
Difficulty: 2
No. of players: Various groups
Material: 4-5 balls per group
Description: The goalie sends balls alternately to the right and left with a low trajectory so that they may be shot by players A and B, etc.

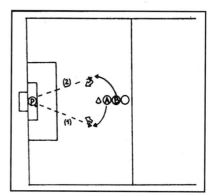

Objective: Shooting: after a forward pass
Difficulty: 2
No. of players: Various groups
Material: 4-5 balls per group
Description: The goalie sends the ball to player A who controls and passes to his teammate B who will have broken away to the right or left and B shoots on goal.

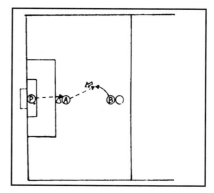

Objective: Shooting: after a forward pass
Difficulty: 3
No. of players: Various groups
Material: 4-5 balls and 3 cones per group
Description: Player A sends balls consecutively to A, B and D so that they are shot to the goal-mouth defended by player P. The exercise is repeated with passes sent by player E.

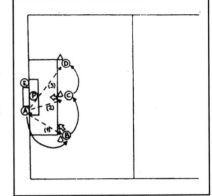

Objective: Shooting: after a forward pass
Difficulty: 3
No. of players: Various groups
Material: 4-5 balls and one cone per group
Description: Player A makes a pass to his team-mate C who is running to meet the pass. C then passes to B who returns it first time for C to shoot.

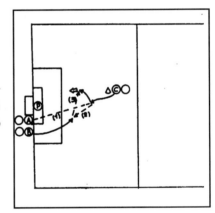

Objective: Shooting: after a forward pass
Difficulty: 3
No. of players: Various groups
Material: 4-5 balls and 3 cones per group
Description: Player B makes a pass to player A who returns it for B to shoot around the 4-man wall.

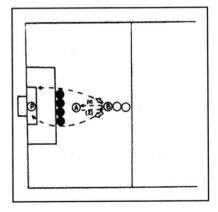

Objective: Shooting: after a forward pass
Difficulty: 3
No. of players: Various groups
Material: 4-5 balls and 3 cones per group
Description: Player A makes a pass to his teammate B who returns it first time for A to shoot. The exercise is repeated from the other side with C and so on.

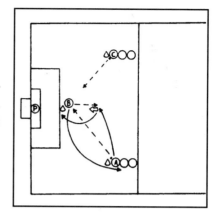

Objective: Shooting: after a forward pass
Difficulty: 3
No. of players: Various groups
Material: 4-5 balls and 3 cones per group
Description: The first player of each group passes the ball to his stationary player and runs around the cone to shoot the return pass.

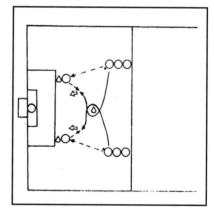

Objective: Shooting: after a forward pass
Difficulty: 4
No. of players: Various groups
Material: 4-5 balls and 3 cones per group
Description: Players are distributed into three groups. Player A sends a ball to his teammate B, who will have made a breaking away move of support; player B passes first time to his teammate C who shoots.

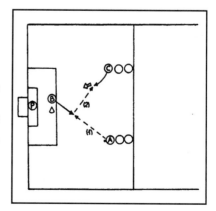

Objective: Shooting: after a forward pass
Difficulty: 4
No. of players: Various groups
Material: 4-5 balls per group
Description: Player A makes a long pass to his teammate B who dribbles toward the front part of the area and leaves the ball for A who has run forward. A then shoots around the wall.

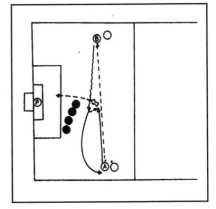

Objective: Shooting: after a forward pass
Difficulty: 4
No. of players: Various groups
Material: 4-5 balls and one cone per group
Description: Player A makes a pass to player B who comes in support, and when he controls the ball, dribbles toward the corner of the area behind the wall. From there he makes a pass backward for A to shoot around or over the wall.

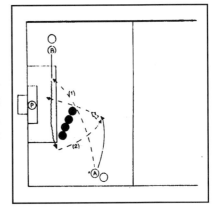

Objective: Shooting: after a forward pass
Difficulty: 4
No. of players: Various groups
Material: 4-5 balls and 1 cone per group
Description: Player A makes a pass to player B who comes in support, and when he controls the ball, dribbles up toward the mid point of the area to make a pass to player C who passes backward for A to shoot around or over the wall.

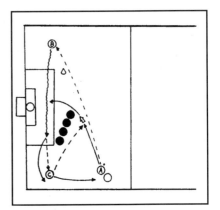

Objective: Shooting: after a forward pass
Difficulty: 4
No. of players: Various groups
Material: 4-5 balls and 6 cones per group
Description: The players are divided into 4 groups. Player A passes the ball to player B who dribbles up to the goal line. From there he sends a pass backward so that player A shoots. The same exercise is repeated on the opposite side with C and D.

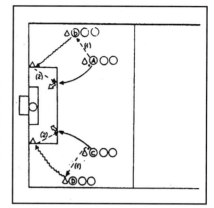

Objective: Shooting: after a forward pass
Difficulty: 4
No. of players: Various groups
Material: 4-5 balls and 5 cones
Description: The players are divided into 4 groups. Player A passes the ball to player B who after controlling the ball makes a pass to player F located at the far post who then passes backward and player A shoots. The same exercise is repeated on the opposite side with C and D.

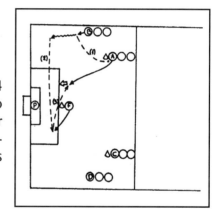

Objective: Shooting: after a forward pass
Difficulty: 3
No. of players: Various groups
Material: 4-5 balls per group
Description: Player A sends a pass to player B who passes to his teammate C in any direction so that he goes after the ball and shoots to the goal defended by player P.

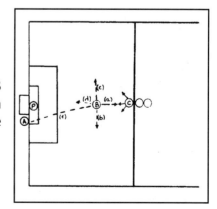

Objective: Shooting: after a forward pass
Difficulty: 3
No. of players: Various groups
Material: 4-5 balls and one cone per group
Description: Player A circles the cone to get the pass from his teammate X to shoot on goal. Then he returns to the starting point to get the second pass from player Y.

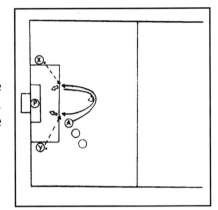

Objective: Shooting: after a forward pass
Difficulty: 3
No. of players: Various groups
Material: 4-5 balls per group
Description: Passes between players A and B who finish with a deep pass from B to A who dribbles and passes backward for B to shoot on the goal defended by P.

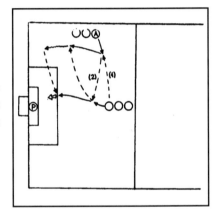

Objective: Shooting: after a forward pass
Difficulty: 3
No. of players: Various groups
Material: 4-5 balls and 3 cones per group
Description: Players are located as the diagram indicates. Player A dribbles from the goal line to the first cone, while his teammate C runs from the goal line to the 2nd cone to circle it, get the pass from A and shoot on goal. The same exercise is done on the other side by B and D.

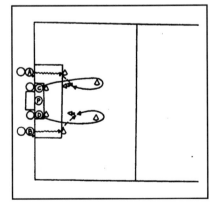

Shooting after a side pass

Objective: Shooting: after a side pass
Difficulty: 3
No. of players: Various groups
Material: 4-5 balls per group
Description: Players A and C make passes toward the center of the field for B to shoot first time over or around the wall.

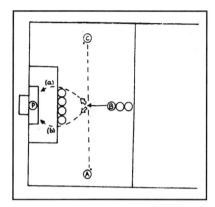

Objective: Shooting: after a side pass.
Difficulty: 3
No. of players: Various groups
Material: 4-5 balls per group
Description: Players A and D make passes toward the center of the field for their team-mates to shoot first time.

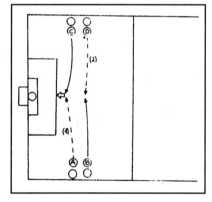

Objective: Shooting: after a side pass
Difficulty: 3
No. of players: Various groups
Material: 4-5 balls per group
Description: Player A passes the ball to his teammate B who makes alternating passes to C and D who shoot on goal.

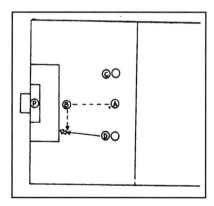

Objective: Shooting: after a side pass
Difficulty: 3
No. of players: Various groups
Material: 4-5 balls per group
Description: Player A makes a pass to teammate B who returns it to him toward the center of the field where player A moves quickly and shoots. The same exercise is repeated on the opposite side. The players exchange positions.

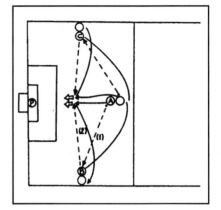

Objective: Shooting: after a side pass
Difficulty: 3
No. of players: Various groups
Material: 4-5 balls and 6 cones per group
Description: Player A passes to player B who dribbles the ball and makes a pass toward the center of the field for player A to shoot. The exercise is repeated on the opposite side. Players exchange their positions.

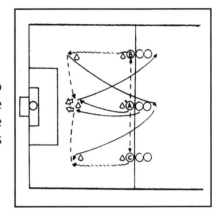

Objective: Shooting: after a side pass
Difficulty: 3
No. of players: Various groups
Material: 4-5 balls per group
Description: Player A makes a pass to B who after getting the ball makes a pass toward the center of the field for player A to shoot after having circled the cone. The exercise is repeated on the opposite side. The players exchange positions.

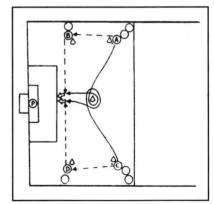

Objective: Shooting: after a side pass
Difficulty: 3
No. of players: Various groups
Material: 4-5 balls per group
Description: Player A dribbles the ball toward the center of the field. B crosses his path, receives the ball and continues the dribble up to the opposite side. After a few yards he makes a crossing pass toward A who dribbles again to be able to make a pass toward the center and B shoots on the goal defended by P.

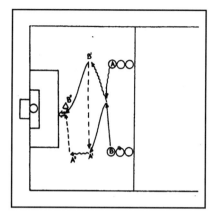

Objective: Shooting: after a side pass
Difficulty: 3
No. of players: Various groups
Material: 4-5 balls per group
Description: The players are divided into 4 groups. Player A dribbles the ball toward the center of the field. Player B crosses his path, receives the ball and continues dribbling toward the opposite side. After a few yards, he makes a pass toward the center so that A shoots on the goal defended by P. The exercise is repeated on the opposite side.

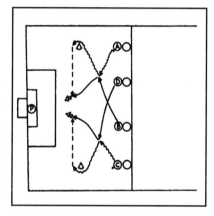

Objective: Shooting: after a side pass
Difficulty: 3
No. of players: Various groups
Material: 4-5 balls per group
Description: Play of side passes and deep passes so that player A who begins the exercise with a pass to B ends with a shot to the goal defended by player P after a side pass from B.

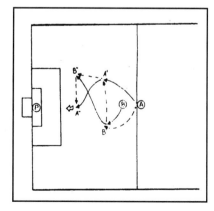

Objective: Shooting: after a side pass
Difficulty: 3
No. of players: Various groups
Material: 4-5 balls per group
Description: Player A makes a pass to his teammate B who dribbles and sends the ball toward A. A then dribbles across the entire field and serves a side pass to B who shoots.

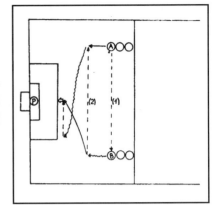

Objective: Shooting: after a side pass
Difficulty: 3
No. of players: Various groups
Material: 4-5 balls and 3 cones per group
Description: Player B dribbles the ball on the diagonal; when he reaches the first cone he makes a pass backward to A and A returns it to him at the second cone. B dribbles again up to the last cone where he serves a side pass to A to shoot.

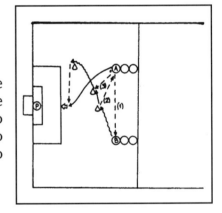

Objective: Shooting: after a side pass
Difficulty: 4
No. of players: Various groups
Material: 4-5 balls and 4 cones per group
Description: Player B after dribbling makes a pass to D who comes in his support; D makes a pass backward for A who makes a deep pass toward C who then passes toward the center of the field for D to shoot before the ball reaches the cone.

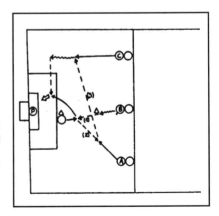

Objective: Shooting: after a side pass
Difficulty: 4
No. of players: Various groups
Material: 4-5 balls and 4 cones per group
Description: Player B, after a dribble, makes a pass to D who is coming in his support. D makes a pass backward to A who makes a deep pass toward C who, when he gets the ball, makes a pass toward the center of the field for D to shoot.

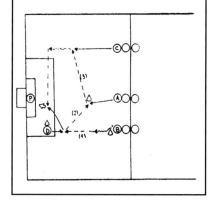

Objective: Shooting: after a side pass
Difficulty: 4
No. of players: Various groups
Material: 4-5 balls and 6 cones per group
Description: The players are divided into four groups. Players A and B play with C and D respectively; they return the ball to them so that they can pass it toward E and F, who when they get the ball dribble and make a pass toward the center so that it may be shot before reaching the cone.

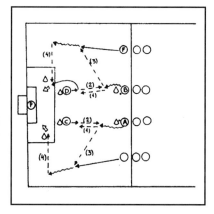

Objective: Shooting: after a side pass
Difficulty: 3
No. of players: Various groups
Material: 4-5 balls per group
Description: Player B passes the ball to his teammate A who dribbles toward the goalmouth. Player B crosses in front of A, gets the ball and dribbles on the diagonal toward the goalmouth. After a few yards, he makes a pass to A who has followed the play so that he can shoot on goal.

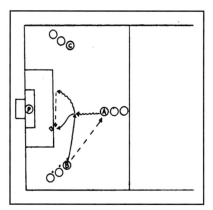

Shooting after a pass from behind

Objective: Shooting: after a back pass
Difficulty: 3
No. of players: Groups of 4-5
Material: 4-5 balls per group
Description: Player A makes a pass from behind
to his teammate B who shoots on goal.

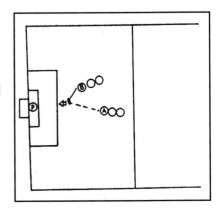

Objective: Shooting: after a back pass
Difficulty: 3
No. of players: Groups of 4-5
Material: 4-5 balls and two cones per group
Description: Player A makes a pass from behind
to his teammate B so that he shoots on the goal
defended by player P; he must do this within the
zone set off by the 2 cones.

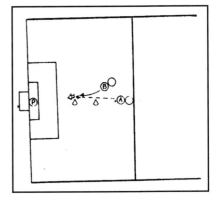

Objective: Shooting: after a back pass
Difficulty: 3
No. of players: Groups of 4-5
Material: 4-5 balls and two cones per group
Description: Player A makes a pass from behind
to his teammate B who shoots from the zone set
off by the cones, going either around or over
the wall.

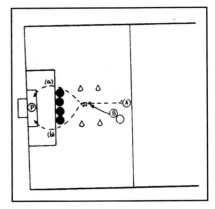

Objective: Shooting: after a back pass
Difficulty: 3
No. of players: Groups of 4-5
Material: 4-5 balls and two cones per group
Description: Player A makes a pass from behind to his teammate B who shoots on the goal defended by player P; he must do this before getting to the 2 cones. The same exercise is repeated on the opposite side.

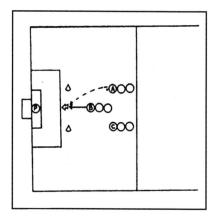

Objective: Shooting: after a back pass
Difficulty: 4
No. of players: Groups of 4-5
Material: 4-5 balls and two cones per group
Description: Player A makes a pass to his teammate C and makes a breaking away movement toward the goal. When player C sees that player A has passed by him and is moving quickly toward the goalmouth, he makes a deep, low pass so that it is shot by A before passing the line of cones. The exercise is repeated on the opposite side.

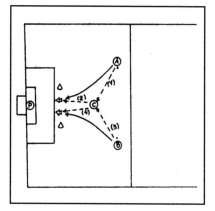

Objective: Shooting: after a back pass
Difficulty: 4
No. of players: Groups of 4-5
Material: 4-5 balls and two cones per group
Description: Passes between players A and B as in the diagram. When player B sees that player A has passed by him and is moving quickly toward the goalmouth, he makes a deep, low pass so that it is shot by A before passing the line of cones. The exercise is repeated on the opposite side.

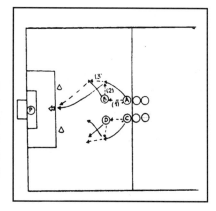

Objective: Shooting: after a back pass
Difficulty: 4
No. of players: Groups of 4-5
Material: 4-5 balls and 2 cones per group
Description: Passes between players A and B as in the diagram; player A dribbles the ball and when he sees that player B has passed by him and is moving quickly toward the goalmouth, he makes a deep, low pass so that it is shot by B before passing the line of cones.

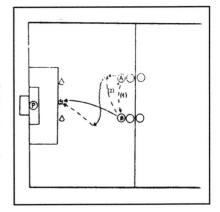

Objective: Shooting: after a back pass
Difficulty: 4
No. of players: Groups of 4–5
Material: 4-5 balls and 2 cones per group
Description: Passes between players A and B as in the diagram; player A dribbles the ball and when he sees that player B has passed by him and is moving quickly toward the goalmouth, he makes a deep, low pass so that it is shot by B before passing the line of cones.

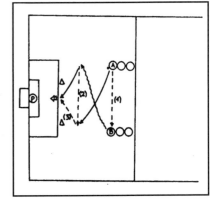

Objective: Shooting: after a back pass
Difficulty: 4
No. of players: Groups of 4-5
Material: 4-5 balls and two cones per group
Description: Passes and dribbling between players A and B as in the diagram. When player A sees that player B has passed by him and is moving quickly to the goalmouth, he makes a deep, low pass so that it is shot by B before passing the line of cones.

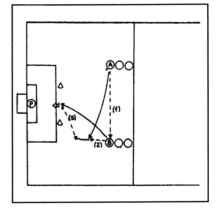

Objective: Shooting: after a pass from behind
Difficulty: 3
No. of players: Groups of 4-5
Material: 4-5 balls and two cones per group
Description: Passes among players A, B and C as in the diagram. When player C sees that player A has passed by him and is moving quickly to the goalmouth, he makes a deep, low pass that is shot by A before passing the line of cones.

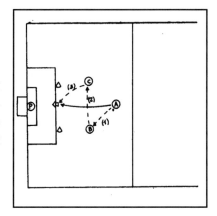

Objective: Shooting: after a pass from behind
Difficulty: 3
No. of players: Groups of 4-5
Material: 4-5 balls and 3 cones per group
Description: Passes between players A and B as in the diagram. When player A sees that player B has passed by him and is moving quickly to the goalmouth, he makes a deep, low pass so that it is shot by B before passing the line of cones. The exercise is repeated on the opposite side.

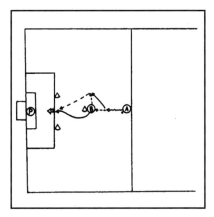

Objective: Shooting: after a pass from behind
Difficulty: 3
No. of players: Groups of 4-5
Material: 4-5 balls and 3 cones per group
Description: Passes between players A and B as in the diagram. When player B sees that player A has passed by him and is moving quickly to the goalmouth, he makes a deep, low pass so that it is shot by A before passing the line of cones. The exercise is repeated on the opposite side.

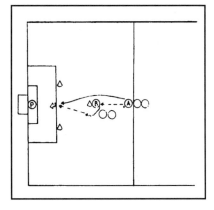

Objective: Shoot after a rear pass
Difficulty: 3
No. of players: Various groups
Material: 4-5 balls per group
Description: Passes among players A, B and C which ending with a deep, low pass for player D's break away move. Player D then shoots on the goal defended by player P. At the same time the same exercise is done on the opposite side.

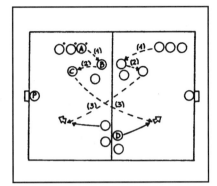

Shooting after receiving

Objective: Shooting: after receiving
Difficulty: 3
No. of players: Groups of 4-5
Material: 4-5 balls and 6 cones per group
Description: Player B runs to the first cone. When he arrives, he receives teammate A's pass, controls and shoots on goal. He goes rapidly to the pivot cone, circles it and runs to the second cone where he receives again the pass from teammate A to control and shoot on goal, etc.

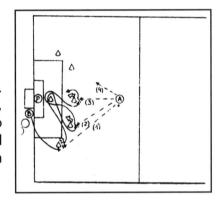

Objective: Shooting: after receiving
Difficulty: 3
No. of players: Groups of 4-5
Material: 5-6 balls and 6 cones per group
Description: Player A runs to the first cone where he receives a pass from P, controls it and shoots on goal. He goes rapidly to the second cone where he receives again, etc.

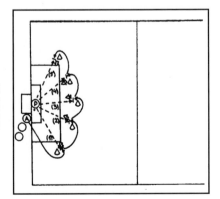

Objective: Shooting: after receiving
Difficulty:
No. of players: Groups of 4-5
Material: 3 balls and 3 cones per group
Description: Player A runs to get the ball that his teammate B passes to him, controls and shoots on goal; he does the same with C, then immediately with D.

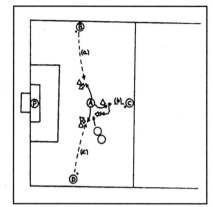

Objective: Shooting: after receiving
Difficulty: 2
No. of players: Groups of 4-5
Material: 4-5 balls per group
Description: Player A sends a ball toward the center of the field; player B runs to control it and shoot on goal.

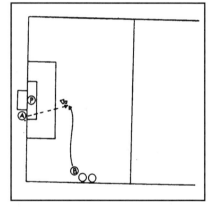

Objective: Shooting: after receiving
Difficulty: 4
No. of players: Various groups
Material: 4-5 balls and 4 cones per group
Description: Players A and B run after the ball that player C has sent to the inside of a zone set out by 4 cones. The first to arrive must control the ball and try to shoot on goal in spite of the opponent's pressure.

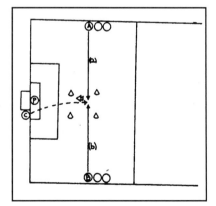

Objective: Shooting: after receiving
Difficulty: 4
No. of players: Groups of 4-5
Material: 4-5 balls and 4 cones per group
Description: The diagram indicates the location of the players. Player A, located in the center of the zone, can receive the pass from any of his teammates without prior notice. He must control and shoot on the goal defended by player P.

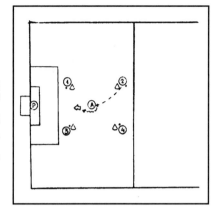

Objective: Shooting: after receiving
Difficulty: 4
No. of players: Groups of 4-5
Material: 4-5 balls and 6 cones per group
Description: Player B passes the ball from the goal line toward a zone set out by 4 cones where player A must try to control the ball and shoot on the goal defended by player P.

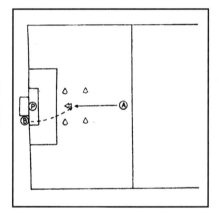

Objective: Shooting: after receiving
Difficulty: 4
No. of players: Groups of 4-5
Material: 4-5 balls and 4 cones per group
Description: Player A makes a deep pass toward a zone marked off by 4 cones. Player B runs after it, gets it and shoots on the goal defended by player P.

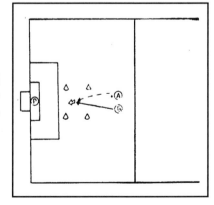

Objective: Shooting: after receiving
Difficulty: 3
No. of players: Groups of 4-5
Material: 4-5 balls and 4 cones per group
Description: Player A makes a lateral pass toward the center of the field toward a zone marked off by 4 cones. Player B runs after it and shoots on the goal defended by player P.

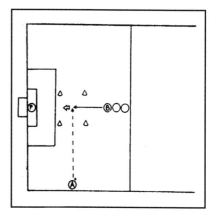

Objective: Shooting: after receiving
Difficulty: 3
No. of players: Groups of 4-5
Material: 4-5 balls and 4 cones per group
Description: Player A makes a diagonal pass toward the center of the field toward a zone marked of by 4 cones. Player B runs after it, gets it, and shoots on the goal defended by player P.

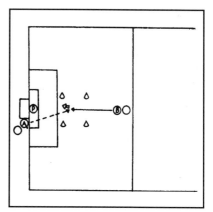

Objective: Shooting: after receiving
Difficulty: 4
No. of players: Various groups
Material: 4-5 balls per group
Description: Player P, with his back to the field of play, sends the ball toward the front part of the area for player A, who must get the ball and shoot to the goal in spite of the opposition of players B and C who come out running from the goal line when P throws the ball.

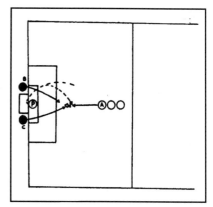

Objective: Shooting: after receiving
Difficulty: 4
No. of players: Various groups
Material: 4-5 balls and 4 cones per group
Description: Player B dribbles the ball and makes a pass to the inside of a zone set off by 4 cones for player A to shoot on goal; at each cone is an X player (defender) who tries to make the shot as difficult as possible for player A.

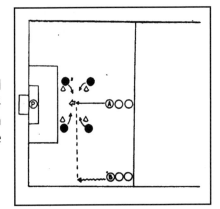

Objective: Shooting: after receiving
Difficulty: 3
No. of players: Groups of 3
Material: One ball and 1 cone per group
Description: Player A passes the ball to teammate B, who with his back to the goalmouth and in front of a cone must receive the ball and shoot on the goal defended by player P. B uses directed control to get into position quickly to shoot.

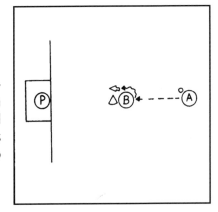

Objective: Shooting: after receiving
Difficulty: 3
No. of players: Groups of 4-5
Material: 4-5 balls per group
Description: Player A dribbles the ball and makes a pass toward the inside of the area where player B has come out from the goal line. There he receives A's pass and shoots on the goal defended by player P.

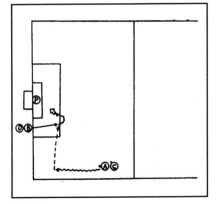

Shooting after a dribble

Objective: Shooting: after a dribble
Difficulty: 2
No. of players: Groups of 3-4
Material: 4-5 balls and one cone per group
Description: Player A makes a diagonal pass to B who controls, dribbles toward the goal and shoots.

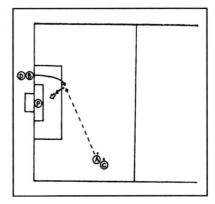

Objective: Shooting: after a dribble
Difficulty: 2
No. of players: Groups of 3
Material: One ball and 2 cones per group
Description: Player A dribbles toward the cone, goes by it to either the left or the right and shoots on the goal defended by P.

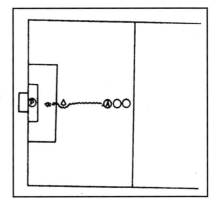

Objective: Shooting: after a dribble
Difficulty: 3
No. of players: Various groups
Material: Two balls per group
Description: Players A and B confront each other to win possession and shoot on the goal defended by player E. If the player who wins possession cannot get by his opponent for a clean shot on goal, he must pass to his teammate (C or D) who then plays 1 v 1 to shoot.

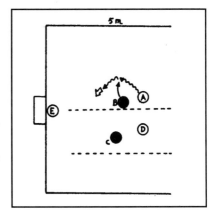

Objective: Shooting: after a dribble
Difficulty: 3
No. of players: Various groups
Material: 4-5 balls and a cone per group
Description: In a reduced area (10 yds), player A dribbles the ball until he runs into opponent B who he must overtake and shoot on goal. Only one try is allowed; if A doesn't manage to shoot after the first dribble, roles are reversed.

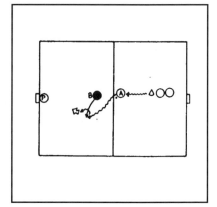

Objective: Shooting: after a dribble
Difficulty: 3
No. of players: Various groups
Material: 4-5 balls and 4 cones per group
Description: Player A must get by defender B and shoot on goal within a zone marked out with 4 cones. This is the same as the previous exercise in that only one attempt to dribble is permitted.

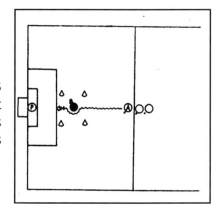

Objective: Shooting: after a dribble
Difficulty: 3
No. of players: Various groups
Material: 4-5 balls and two cones per group
Description: Player A makes a pass to B and B returns it to him. On the return pass, defending player C comes out from the goal line to meet A who must get by him and shoot on goal. Only one attempt to dribble is allowed.

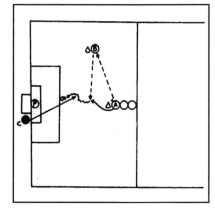

Objective: Shooting: after a dribble
Difficulty: 3
No. of players: Various groups
Material: 4-5 balls per group
Description: The goalie throws the ball toward the center of the field. Two players run after it; the player who wins possession attacks the goal and the other defends. Only one attempt to dribble is allowed.

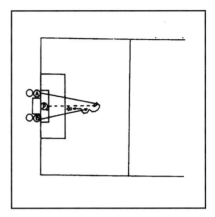

Objective: Shooting: after a dribble
Difficulty: 2
No. of players: Various groups
Material: One ball and 4 cones per group
Description: Players A and B play 1 v 1 to try to shoot on the small goals defended by two team-mates from each team.

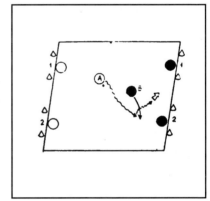

Objective: Shooting: after a dribble
Difficulty: 2
No. of players: Various groups
Material: 4-5 balls and 3 cones per group
Description: Player A makes a pass to teammate B. Player D tries to prevent B from shooting on goal. The exercise is repeated on the opposite side.

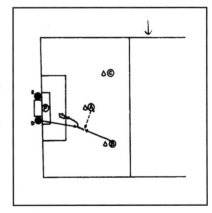

Objective: Shooting: after a dribble
Difficulty: 3
No. of players: Various groups
Material: 4-5 balls and one cone per group
Description: Player P sends a pass to player A who dribbles rapidly toward the goalmouth and must avoid player B's defense to shoot.

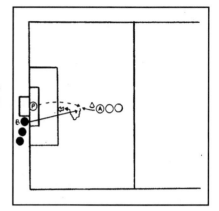

Objective: Shooting: after a dribble
Difficulty: 3
No. of players: Various groups
Material: 4-5 balls per group
Description: Player E sends a pass to player A who dribbles rapidly toward the goalmouth and must avoid player B's defense to shoot. They play simultaneously on both sides. Reduced area.

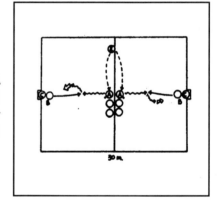

Objective: Shooting: after a dribble
Difficulty: 3
No. of players: Various groups
Material: 4-5 balls and 3 cones per group
Description: Player A dribbles the ball around all the cones and confronts B in a 1 v 1 to shoot on the goal defended by C. Only one attempt to get by the defender is allowed.

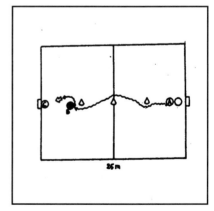

Objective: Shooting: after a dribble
Difficulty: 3
No. of players: Various groups
Material: 4-5 balls per group
Description: Player P throws the ball toward coach E. Players B and C run toward E. Halfway there they wait for the pass from E who can go to either of the two. The player who does not receive the pass must try to avoid the shot by the player who does.

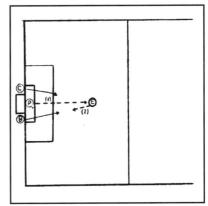

Objective: Shooting: after a dribble
Difficulty: 1
No. of players: Groups of 6-8
Material: 3-4 balls and 3 cones per group
Description: The players are divided into 3 groups and dribble up to the cone, make a move to either the left or the right as per the coach's instruction and shoot on goal.

Objective: Shooting: after a dribble
Difficulty: 2
No. of players: Groups of 2
Material: One ball per group
Description: Player A sends the ball to B who returns it to him and goes out to defend him. A tries to beat B and shoot on goal.

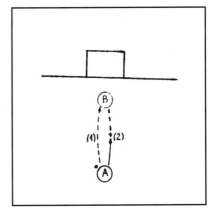

Objective: Shooting: after a dribble
Difficulty: 3
No. of players: Groups of 5-6
Material: 3-4 balls per group
Description: Player A passes the ball to B who gets it and faces A, who has gone out to meet him, in a 1 v 1 to shoot on goal.

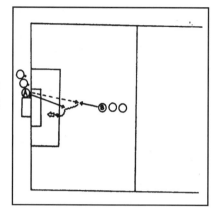

Objective: Shooting: after a dribble
Difficulty: 4
No. of players: Groups of 5-6
Material: 2-3 balls and 4 cones per group
Description: Player A dribbles the ball until running into B within a square 10 x 10 yard zone. He must try to dribble by B and shoot on goal without leaving the zone.

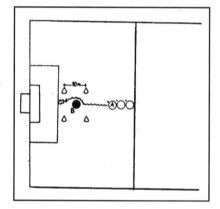

Objective: Shooting: after a dribble
Difficulty: 3
No. of players: Groups of 6-8
Material: 3-4 balls and two cones per group
Description: The players are divided into two groups at each side of the area. At the signal A and B run toward their respective cones, receive the pass from E, turn, dribble and shoot on goal.

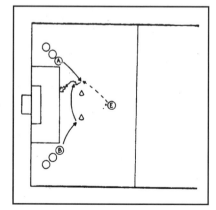

Objective: Shooting: after a dribble
Difficulty: 2
No. of players: Groups of 6-8
Material: 3-4 balls and two cones per group
Description: In an area 20 yards long players play 3 v 3 with one ball per pair (3 x 1 v 1). Each player defends his goal and attacks the opposite goal.

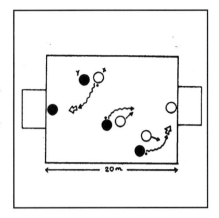

Objective: Shooting: after a dribble
Difficulty: 4
No. of players: Groups of 6-8
Material: 3-4 balls per group
Description: In an area 20 yards long players play 3 v 3 with one ball per pair (3 x 1 v 1). Each time a player scores, his defender is eliminated and he supports his teammates.

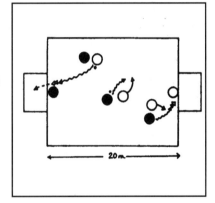

Objective: Shooting: after a dribble
Difficulty: 3
No. of players: Groups of 7
Material: One ball and two cones per group
Description: One goal defended by a neutral player is attacked by two teams of 4 players. Each player attempts to shoot on goal after dribbling by his defender and if he needs help can use his teammates.

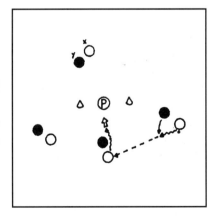

Objective: Shooting: after a dribble
Difficulty: 4
No. of players: Groups of 6
Material: One ball per group
Description: The goalie passes the ball to his teammate A who must attempt to beat his defender and pass to B who, when he receives must try to shoot on goal in spite of the opposition.

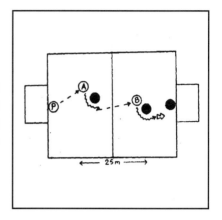

Objective: Shooting: after a dribble
Difficulty: 3
No. of players: Groups of 8-10
Material: 3-4 balls per group
Description: In an area 20 yards long, the coach sends a ball toward the center of the field. Two players run toward him and the one who wins possession becomes the offensive player and the other the defensive player in a 1 v 1 to shoot on goal.

Objective: Shooting: after a dribble
Difficulty: 2
No. of players: Groups of 5-6
Material: 2-3 balls and 4-5 cones per group
Description: Player A dribbles the ball going around the cones with the dribbling technique called by the coach. At the coach's signal, the player must shoot on goal.

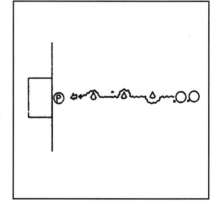

Objective: Shooting: after a dribble
Difficulty: 3
No. of players: Groups of 8-10
Material: 4-5 balls per group
Description: Player A dribbles the ball until running into the two defenders who cut him off. At this point he makes a pass to the right or to the left so that his teammate dribbles by the defender who has gone to meet him and shoots on goal.

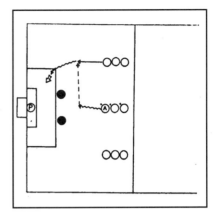

Objective: Shooting: after a dribble
Difficulty: 4
No. of players: Groups of 8-10
Material: 4-5 balls per group
Description: Players are divided into 3 groups. Each player has 15 seconds to dribble and shoot on goal. If he doesn't manage to beat the defender in the 15 seconds, he loses the option to shoot.

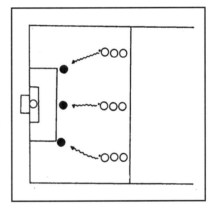

Objective: Shooting: after a dribble
Difficulty: 3
No. of players: Groups of 4
Material: One ball per group
Description: Two attackers against two defenders. A and B can make as many passes as they want but they can only shoot on goal after beating a defender with a dribble.

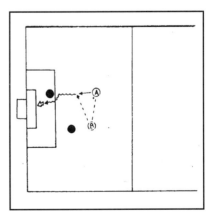

Objective: Shooting: after a dribble
Difficulty: 3
No. of players: Groups of 4
Material: One ball per group
Description: Player A attempts to beat his defender and shoot on goal. If he can't get by him, he can make a pass to his teammate B who tries to score in the other goal. When a player passes to his teammate, he switches to defense.

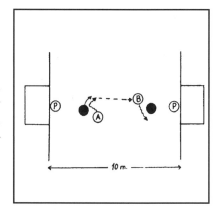

Shooting after a centering pass

Objective: Shooting: after a centering pass
Difficulty: 3
No. of players: Various groups
Material: 4-5 balls per group
Description: Player A makes a pass to teammate B who dribbles and makes a deep pass to C. C makes a pass backward to player A who crosses for B to shoot on goal.

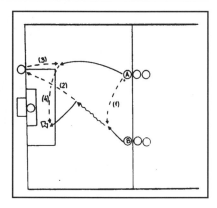

Objective: Shooting: after a centering pass
Difficulty: 3
No. of players: Various groups
Material: 4-5 balls per group
Description: Passes among players A, B and C; when C receives the ball, he dribbles it and makes an cross for his teammates to try to shoot on the goal defended by P.

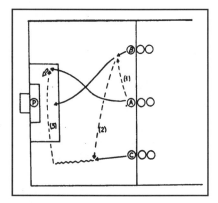

Objective: Shooting: after a centering pass
Difficulty: 3
No. of players: Various groups
Material: 4-5 balls per group
Description: Player A makes crosses from the corner. Player B attempts to shoot on the goal defended by P.

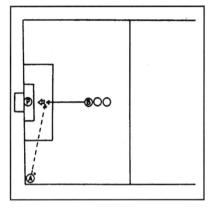

Objective: Shooting: after a centering pass
Difficulty: 3
No. of players: Various groups
Material: 4-5 balls per group
Description: Passes and criss-crossing between players A and B down the wing. Finally player A makes a cross into the goalmouth for B to shoot on goal. The exercise is repeated down the opposite side by players C and D.

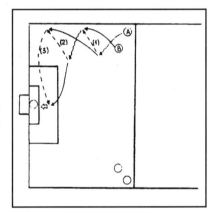

Objective: Shooting: after a centering pass
Difficulty: 3
No. of players: Various groups
Material: 4-5 balls per group
Description: Passes and spreading out/splitting between players A and B down the wing. Finally player A makes a cross into the goalmouth for B to shoot on goal. The exercise is repeated down the opposite side by players C and D.

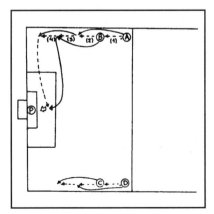

Objective: Shooting: after a centering pass
Difficulty: 3
No. of players: Various groups
Material: 4-5 balls per group
Description: Play of forward and lateral passes between players A and B down the wing. Finally player B crosses into the goalmouth for A to shoot on goal. The action is repeated down the opposite side by players C and D.

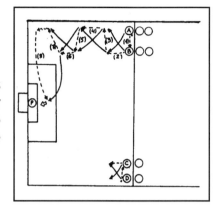

Objective: Shooting: after a centering pass.
Difficulty: 3
No. of players: Various groups
Material: 4-5 balls per group
Description: Play of lateral passes between players A, B and C. Player C, after dribbling, crosses into the goalmouth to players A and B, who have criss-crossed and try to shoot on goal.

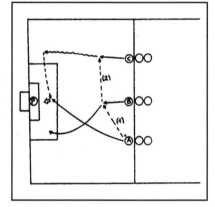

Objective: Shooting: after a centering pass
Difficulty: 3
No. of players: Various groups
Material: 4-5 balls per group
Description: Play of lateral, front and penetrating passes among players A, B and C. At the end, player A, after dribbling, crosses into the goalmouth to players B and C, who have criss-crossed and try to shoot on goal.

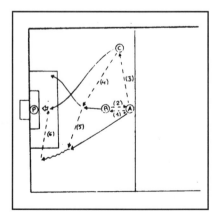

Objective: Shooting: after centering pass
Difficulty: 3
No. of players: Various groups
Material: 4-5 balls per group
Description: Play of side, front and penetrating passes among players A, B and C; At the end, player C crosses into the goalmouth to players A and B who try to shoot on goal.

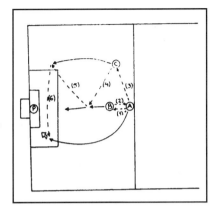

Objective: Shooting: after a centering pass
Difficulty: 3
No. of players: Various groups
Material: 4-5 balls per group
Description: Play of lateral, frontal and deep passes among players A, B and C; at the end player C, after dribbling, crosses into the goalmouth to players A and B who try to shoot on goal.

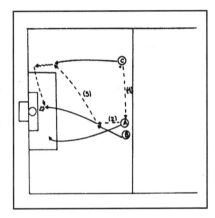

Objective: Shooting: after a centering pass
Difficulty: 3
No. of players: Various groups
Material: 4-5 balls per group
Description: Play of lateral, front and penetrating passes among players A, B, and C; at the end player B, after dribbling, crosses into the goalmouth to players A and C who try to shoot on goal.

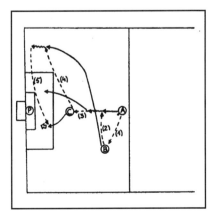

Objective: Shooting: after a centering pass
Difficulty: 3
No. of players: Various groups
Material: 4-5 balls per group
Description: Passes among players A, B and C finishing with a deep pass to C who, after controlling, dribbles the ball and makes a cross for his teammates A and B who try to shoot on goal.

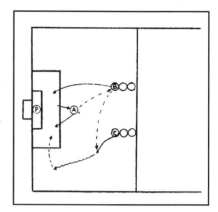

Shooting after a wall pass

Objective: Shooting: after a wall pass
Difficulty: 3
No. of players: Various groups
Material: 4-5 balls per group
Description: Players A and D dribble the ball toward the cone, play a wall pass with B and C who have come out from the goal line and shoot first time on goal.

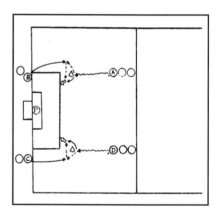

Objective: Shooting: after a wall pass
Difficulty: 3
No. of players: Various groups
Material: 4-5 balls per group
Description: Player A dribbles the ball and at each cone plays a wall pass with teammates B and C to shoot on the goal defended by P. The exercise is done at the same time on both sides.

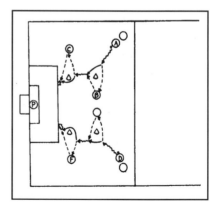

Objective: Shooting: after a wall pass
Difficulty: 3
No. of players: Various groups
Material: 4-5 balls and 4 cones per group
Description: Player A passes the ball to his teammate B and makes a breaking away movement to receive the return pass from B; A then plays a wall pass with B, so that B can shoot on the goal defended by P.

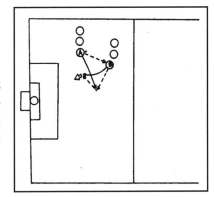

Objective: Shooting: after a wall pass
Difficulty: 3
No. of players: Various groups
Material: 4-5 balls per group
Description: Player A plays a wall pass with B, dribbles, plays another wall pass with C and shoots first time on goal.

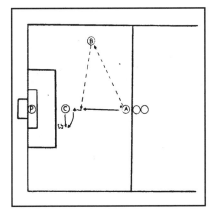

Objective: Shooting: after a wall pass
Difficulty: 3
No. of players: Various groups
Material: 4-5 balls per group
Description: Player A plays a forward pass to his teammate B, who after returning A's pass runs to the free space created at his back, receives A's pass and shoots on goal.

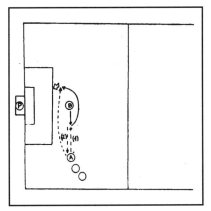

Objective: Shooting: after a wall pass
Difficulty: 3
No. of players: Various groups
Material: 4-5 balls and two cones per group
Description: Player B receives a long pass from teammate A; he controls, dribbles, plays a wall pass with teammates C and D and shoots on goal. The same exercise is done on both sides.

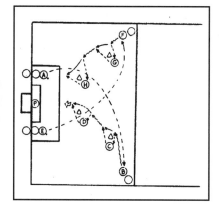

Objective: Shooting: after a wall pass
Difficulty: 3
No. of players: Various groups
Material: 4-5 balls per group
Description: Player B receives a long pass from teammate A, controls, dribbles, plays a wall pass with C and shoots on goal. The same exercise is done on both sides.

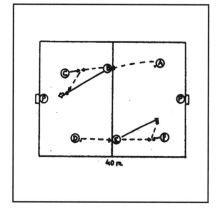

Objective: Shooting: after a wall pass
Difficulty: 3
No. of players: Various groups
Material: 4-5 balls and two cones per group
Description: Player A dribbles the ball up to the cone, plays a wall pass with B and shoots on goal. The same exercise is done on both sides.

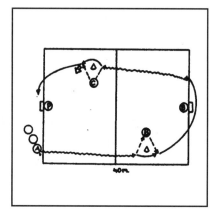

Objective: Shooting: after a wall pass
Difficulty: 3
No. of players: Various groups
Material: 4-5 balls per group
Description: Player A sends a long pass to B who controls and dribbles toward the goalmouth. Player A, after passing, runs in support of his teammate to play a wall pass with him. Player B, after the wall pass, shoots on goal.

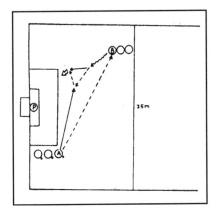

Objective: Shooting: after a wall pass
Difficulty: 3
No. of players: Various groups
Material: 4-5 balls per group
Description: Exercise similar to the previous one but with opposition. Player A sends a long pass to B who controls and dribbles toward the goalmouth. Player A, after passing, runs in support of his teammate to play a wall pass with him. Player B, after the wall pass, shoots on goal.

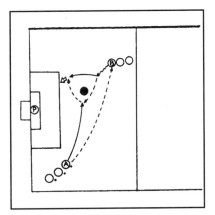

Objective: Shooting: after a wall pass
Difficulty: 3
No. of players: Various groups
Material: 4-5 balls per group
Description: Player A passes to B who dribbles, makes a penetrating pass into the run of C and runs inside toward the goalmouth. Player C makes a heel pass, returning the ball to B who shoots on goal.

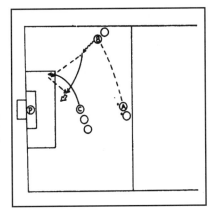

Objective: Shooting: after a wall pass
Difficulty: 3
No. of players: 3
Material: 4-5 balls per group
Description: Player A dribbles the ball and gets the support of player B who instead of returning the ball to player A, sends it to C who continues the play on the opposite side.

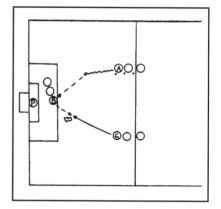

Objective: Shooting: after a wall pass
Difficulty: 3
No. of players: 3
Material: 4-5 balls per group
Description: Players are located as the diagram indicates. Players A and B play a wall pass together. After the wall pass, Player A sends a long ball toward C who shoots on goal.

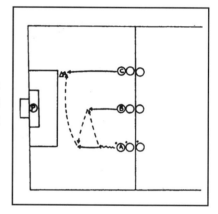

Objective: Shooting: after a wall a pass
Difficulty: 3
No. of players: Various groups
Material: 4-5 balls per group
Description: Player A sends a pass to B who plays a wall pass with C. C, instead of returning it to B, passes it to A who has continued the play on the opposite side and A shoots on goal.

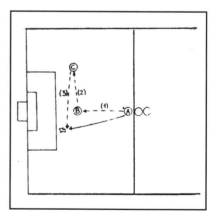

Volley shots and Half-volley shots

Objective: Volleys and Half Volleys
Difficulty: 3
No. of players: Groups of 3
Material: per group ball per group
Description: Player A sends a pass to B. B lets the ball bounce and shoots on goal with a half-volley or takes the ball out of the air on the full volley.

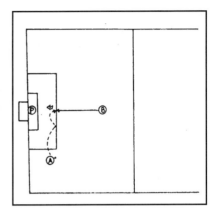

Objective: Volleys and Half Volleys
Difficulty: 3
No. of players: Groups of 3
Material: per group ball per group
Description: Player A, positioned behind player B, sends a pass over B's head; B lets the ball bounce and shoots on goal with a half-volley or takes the ball out of the air on the full volley.

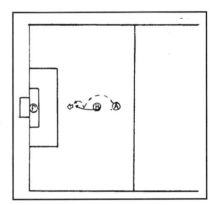

Objective: Volleys and Half Volleys
Difficulty: 3
No. of players: Groups of 3
Material: per group ball per group
Description: The goalie throws the ball with a parabolic trajectory toward player A. A lets it bounce and shoots on goal with a half-volley or takes the ball out of the air on the full volley.

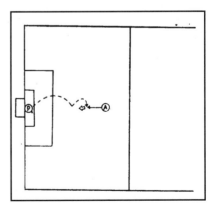

Objective: Volleys and Half Volleys
Difficulty: 3
No. of players: Groups of 3
Material: One ball per group
Description: Player A makes a pass to B; B returns it to him by means of a deep pass with a parabolic trajectory. Player A runs after the ball and after a bounce shoots on goal with a half-volley or takes the ball out of the air on the full volley.

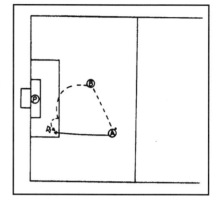

Objective: Volleys and Half Volleys
Difficulty: 3
No. of players: Groups of 3
Material: One ball per group
Description: Player A makes a pass to B; B returns it to him by means of a lateral pass with a parabolic trajectory. Player A runs after the ball and after a bounce shoots on goal with a half-volley or takes the ball out of the air on the full volley.

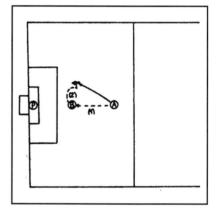

Objective: Volleys and Half Volleys
Difficulty: 3
No. of players: Groups of 4
Material: One ball per group
Description: Player A makes a frontal pass to player B; B passes the ball toward player C who is located in a wide position. From there, player C sends a deep pass to A who shoots on goal with a half-volley or volley.

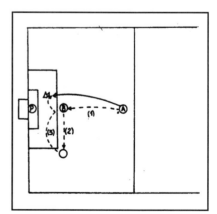

Objective: Volleys and Half Volleys
Difficulty: 3
No. of players: Groups of 3
Material: One ball per group
Description: Player A sends a ball to B over the goal. Player B runs after it and shoots on goal with a half-volley or volley.

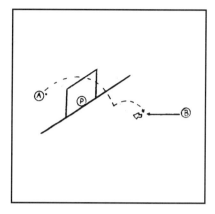

Objective: Volleys and Half Volleys
Difficulty: 3
No. of players: Various groups
Material: 4-5 balls and 4 cones per group
Description: Player B sends a long and deep pass to C; C makes a pass toward the center of the field where player E thrusts forward to shoot on goal with a half-volley or volley. The same exercise is repeated on the opposite side (players A and D.)

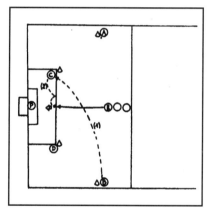

Objective: Volleys and Half Volleys
Difficulty: 3
No. of players: Various groups
Material: 3-4 balls per group
Description: Player A sends a long and deep pass to B; B sends a pass toward the center of the field where player A shoots on goal with a half-volley or volley.

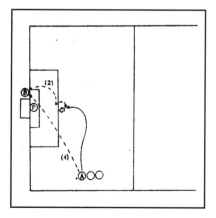

Application plays

Objective: Shooting: Application plays
Difficulty: 3
No. of players: Various groups
Material: One ball per group
Description: Two teams play 5 v 5 on a reduced field. Each chance that the players have to shoot on goal must be taken advantage of no matter what position the player with the ball is playing at that time.

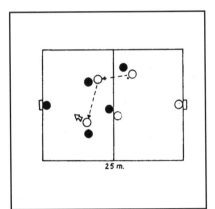

Objective: Shooting: Application plays
Difficulty: 3
No. of players: Various groups
Material: One ball and 8 cones per group
Description: Two teams play 5 v 5 on a reduced field. The diagram indicates the position of the players. Players must shoot from outside the 6 yd line and they can score in any of the 3 goals marked off with cones that are defended by two players from each team.

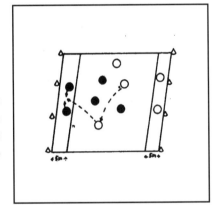

Objective: Shooting: Application plays
Difficulty: 3
No. of players: Various groups
Material: Two balls per player and a medicine ball
Description: The two teams positioned as in the diagram must shoot against the medicine ball which is located in the center of the field to send it into the opponent's area.

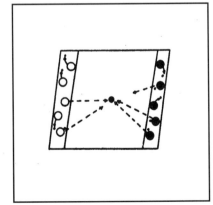

Objective: Shooting: Application plays
Difficulty: 3
No. of players: Various players
Material: Two balls per group
Description: Two teams of 3, positioned as in the diagram, must shoot at the opposite goal. The defending team cannot pass the line marked at some 5 yards from the goal to defend it. The defenders can only make 2 touches to the ball; the 1st to control the opposing team's shot and the 2nd to shoot.

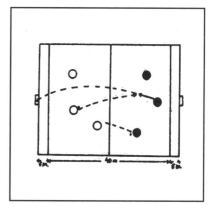

Objective: Shooting: Application plays
Difficulty: 3
No. of players: Various groups
Material: 4 balls and 8 cones per group
Description: Two teams of 3, positioned as in the diagram, must shoot to the opposite zone, trying to hit the cones which the other team tries to defend.

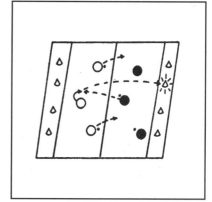

Objective: Shooting: Application plays
Difficulty: 3
No. of players: Various groups
Material: One ball per player and 6 hoops
Description: Each player has a ball and shoots on goal, trying to shoot through the hoops hanging from the crossbar. Each hoop has a value; after 5 shots by each player, the one with the most points wins.

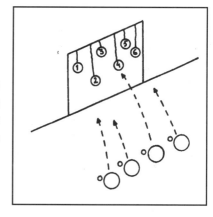

Objective: Shooting: Application plays
Difficulty: 3
No. of players: Various groups
Material: One ball per player
Description: All players are located along the edge of the central circle as in the diagram and must shoot on the goal defended by player P. Shots are made in numerical order, one team after another. The team with the most goals wins.

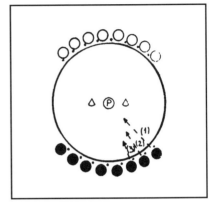

Objective: Shooting: Application plays
Difficulty: 3
No. of players: Various groups
Material: 5-6 balls and 6-8 cones per group
Description: Teams are positioned as the diagram indicates. Players Y shoot on the goals defended by players X. The team with the most goals wins.

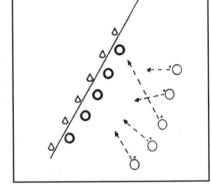

Objective: Shooting: Application plays
Difficulty: 3
No. of players: Various groups
Material: 5-6 balls and two ropes per group
Description: Teams are positioned as the diagram indicates. Players from both teams pass the ball among themselves. At the coach's signal the player who possesses the ball at that time shoots on goal. The team with the most goals wins.

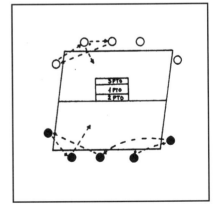

Objective: Shooting: Application plays
Difficulty: 3
No. of players: Various groups
Material: One ball, 4 cones and 2 hoops per group
Description: Two teams of 6 players play among themselves. In each goalmouth there are 2 hoops with a 3-point value and 2 cones with a 2-point value; the rest of the goalmouth carries a 1 point value. The team with the most points wins.

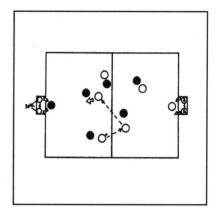

Objective: Shooting: Application plays
Difficulty: 3
No. of players: Various groups
Material: 4 balls and 4 cones per group
Description: In a zone marked with cones outside the penalty area, the players dribble their ball. When the coach calls a number, that player must shoot on goal.

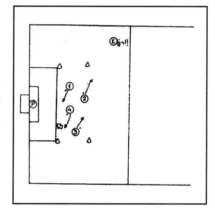

Objective: Shooting: Application plays
Difficulty: 3
No. of players: Various groups
Material: One ball per group
Description: Two teams face off attempting to score in the opposing team's goal; players can't shoot unless they first make a wall pass.

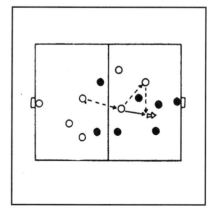

Objective: Shooting: Application plays
Difficulty: 3
No. of players: Various groups
Material: One ball per group
Description: Two teams face off trying to score in the opposing team's goal. In each corner, an attacker is positioned in a marked zone. For a goal to count, the ball must have passed through one of these zones.

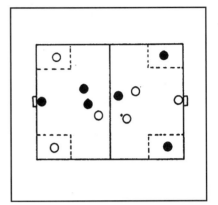

Objective: Shooting: Application plays
Difficulty: 3
No. of players: Various groups
Material: One ball per group
Description: Two teams face off trying to score in the opposing team's goal; in front of each goalmouth there is a line that marks the shooting area. All shots must be taken from outside this line.

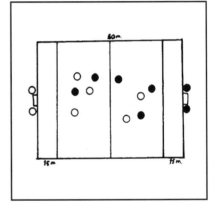

CHAPTER 7

HEADING
Exercises for movement coordination

Objective: Movement coordination
Difficulty: 2
No. of players: Various players
Material: One ball per player
Description: Each player attempts to keep the ball in the air as long as possible with successive head touches.

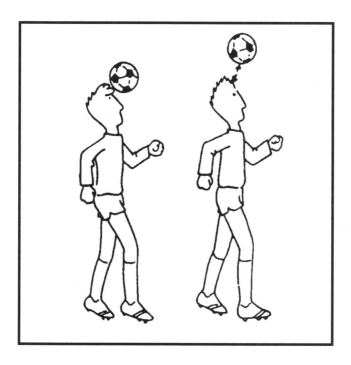

Objective: Movement coordination
Difficulty: 1
No. of players: Groups of 2
Material: One ball per pair
Description: Players A and B pass the ball to each other with their head as many times as possible.

Objective: Movement coordination
Difficulty: 3
No. of players: Groups of 2
Material: One ball per pair
Description: Player A makes a pass with his head to B after having made a vertical touch.

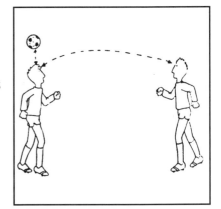

Objective: Movement coordination
Difficulty: 2
No. of players: Groups of 2
Material: One ball per pair
Description: Player B makes a pass with his head to A and makes a complete revolution. A makes as many touches with his head as is necessary before passing the ball back to B.

Objective: Movement coordination
Difficulty: 3
No. of players: Groups of 2
Material: One ball per pair
Description: Player B passes the ball with his head to A, sits down and gets up again. A makes as many touches with his head as is necessary before passing the ball back to B.

Objective: Movement coordination
Difficulty: 2
No. of players: Groups of 2
Material: One ball per group
Description: Player B is stretched out on the floor and comes up to head the balls sent by his teammate A. The movement involves raising the trunk and head to go after the ball (like a sit-up).

Objective: Movement coordination
Difficulty: 4
No. of players: Groups of 4
Material: One ball per group
Description: Players B and C exchange positions after heading the ball to A and D. A and D make successive touches with their head to keep the ball in the air until their teammates are in position.

Objective: Movement coordination
Difficulty: 4
No. of players: Groups of 3
Material: One ball per group
Description: Player A sends the ball to B, turns, heads the ball to C, turns, heads the ball again to B and so on. B and C keep the ball in the air with their heads while waiting for A to turn for their pass.

Objective: Movement coordination
Difficulty: 4
No. of players: Groups of 3
Material: One ball and one hurdle per group
Description: Similar to the previous exercise, except this time, Player A must jump over a hurdle each time he turns to receive the next pass. This should force B and C to keep the ball up for a longer period of time.

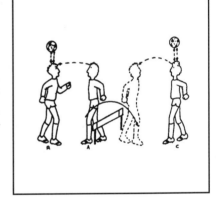

Objective: Movement coordination
Difficulty: 1
No. of players: Groups of 2
Material: One ball per group
Description: Player A holds a ball in his hand with his arm extended. Player B runs toward him and jumps to head the ball.

Objective: Movement coordination
Difficulty: 1
No. of players: Groups of 2
Material: One ball per group, a chair or similar object
Description: Player A, standing on a box, holds a ball in both hands with his arms extended. Player B runs toward him and jumps to head the ball.

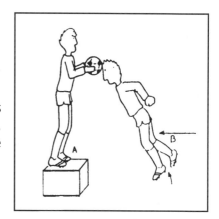

Objective: Movement coordination
Difficulty: 1
No. of players: Groups of 3
Material: two balls per group
Description: Player A holds a ball in each hand with his arms extended; players B and C run toward him and jump to head the ball.

Objective: Movement coordination
Difficulty: 1
No. of players: Groups of 2
Material: One ball per group
Description: Player A holds the ball in the air with both hands; player B runs toward him and jumps to head the ball, trying to knock it out of player A's hands.

Objective: Movement coordination
Difficulty: 3
No. of players: groups of 5
Material: 4 balls per group
Description: A group of 4 players, each one with a ball, forms a circle. In the center player E heads the balls sent to him by his teammates.

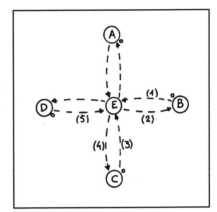

Objective: Movement coordination
Difficulty: 2
No. of players: Groups of 2
Material: One ball and two cones per group
Description: Player A sends the ball to B who shoots with his head on the goal defended by A.

Objective: Movement coordination
Difficulty: 3
No. of players: Groups of 2
Material: One ball and 4 cones per group
Description: Player A throws the ball in the air to himself and with his head tries to score in the goal defended by B.

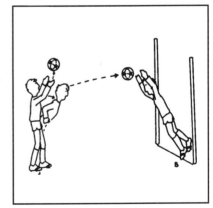

Objective: Movement coordination
Difficulty: 2
No. of players: Groups of 2
Material: One ball and one flag per group
Description: Player B keeps the ball up with his head while B runs around a small flag located 3 yards away. When B returns, A heads the ball to him, B heads it back and runs around the flag again.

Objective: Movement coordination
Difficulty: 4
No. of players: Groups of 2
Material: One ball and two cones per group
Description: Same as the previous exercise except both players, after passing the ball, run around a flag.

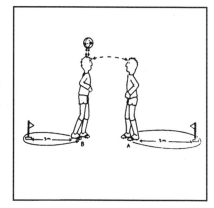

Objective: Movement coordination
Difficulty: 4
No. of players: Groups of 8
Material: 4 balls and one flag per group
Description: The outside players, after receiving the ball, make as many touches as necessary to allow their teammates to go around the center flag.

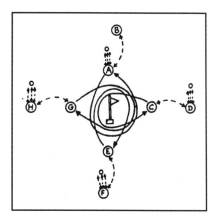

Objective: Movement coordination
Difficulty: 2
No. of players: Groups of 3
Material: One ball per group
Description: Player A heads the ball to B who turns toward C while juggling with his head and heads to C. C returns it first time and the exercise continues.

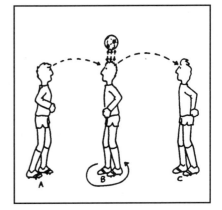

Objective: Movement coordination
Difficulty: 3
No. of players: Groups of 2
Material: One ball per group
Description: Players A and B pass the ball back and forth with their heads while B retreats and A follows.

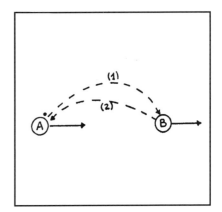

Objective: Movement coordination
Difficulty: 4
No. of players: Groups of 2
Material: One ball per group
Description: Player B heads to A who returns it to him with a half-volley.

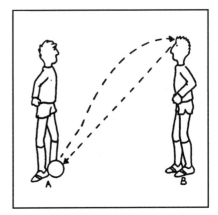

Objective: Movement coordination
Difficulty: 4
No. of players: Groups of 3
Material: One ball per group
Description: Player A heads to B who returns it to him; A's next pass goes to C who passes to B who has made a half turn to repeat the process.

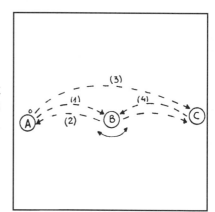

Objective: Movement coordination
Difficulty: 2
No. of players: Groups of 3
Material: One ball per group
Description: Player A heads the ball toward B who flicks the ball on to C with a header; C heads it back to B who flicks to A and so on.

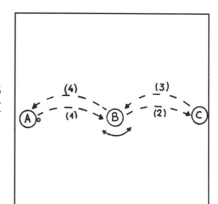

Objective: Movement coordination
Difficulty: 2
No. of players: Groups of 3
Material: One ball per group
Description: Player B hits the ball with his head toward A who with a header returns it to C while B runs to occupy A's place.

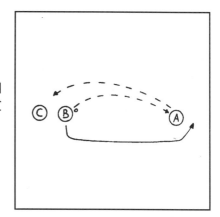

Objective: Movement coordination
Difficulty: 4
No. of players: Groups of 3
Material: One ball per group
Description: All players play only with their heads. One outside player sends the ball to the inside of the circle to B and moves into B's position; B sends to C and moves into C's position, etc.

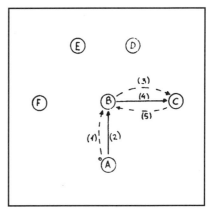

Objective: Movement coordination
Difficulty: 4
No. of players: Groups of 3
Material: One ball per group
Description: All players play only with their heads. Player A sends to B who returns it to him; A then sends a long pass to C who in turn plays short with B and long with A, etc.

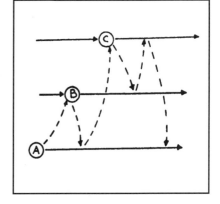

Objective: Movement coordination
Difficulty: 3
No. of players: Groups of 4
Material: One ball and 4 cones per group
Description: Divided in groups of 2 the players defend and attack their respective goals. One of the pair serves to his teammate who shoots on the goal defended by the opposing pair.

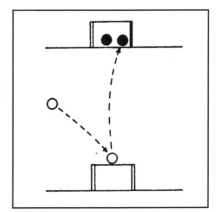

Objective: Movement coordination
Difficulty: 3
No. of players: Groups of 4
Material: Two balls per group
Description: Players A, B, C, and D, located on the corners of a square, make passes among themselves with a diagonal trajectory.

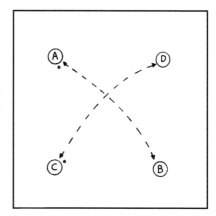

Objective: Movement coordination
Difficulty: 3
No. of players: Various groups
Material: Two balls and one cone per group
Description: Player C sends a long pass. Player X, departing from the cone, runs to intercept it and with a header passes to B who sends it again to player C. At the same time, and on the opposite side, player A has sent a long pass so that X also goes to intercept and heads toward D.

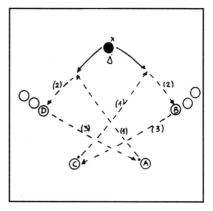

Exercises for understanding (recognizing) trajectories

Objective: Understanding trajectories
Difficulty: 1
No. of players: Groups of 2
Material: One ball per group
Description: Player A throws a high bounce pass for B to head.

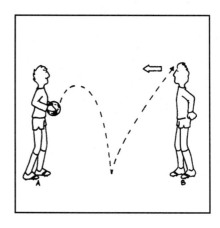

Objective: Understanding trajectories
Difficulty: 2
No. of players: Groups of 4 or 5
Material: One ball and one bench per group
Description: Player B throws a ball toward A who jumps over the bench and while in the air heads the ball back to B.

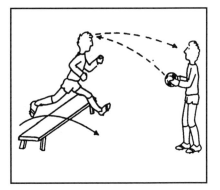

Objective: Understanding trajectories
Difficulty: 1
No. of players: Groups of 2
Material: One ball per group
Description: Player A, with his back to his teammate B, turns around at B's signal and heads the ball back to B.

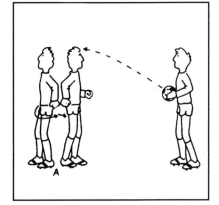

Objective: Understanding trajectories
Difficulty: 3
No. of players: Groups of 4 or 5
Material: One ball and one bench per group
Description: Player A with his back to his teammate B, turns around at B's signal and jumps over the bench to head the ball back to B.

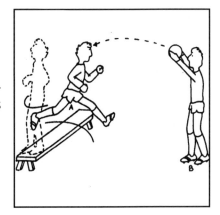

Objective: Understanding trajectories
Difficulty: 2
No. of players: Groups of 5-6
Material: Supports/stands, rope, and one ball per group
Description: The group of players, positioned in rows, in turn run and jump to head the pass from their teammate back over the rope.

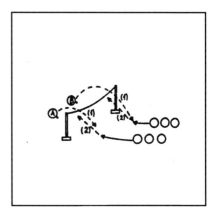

Objective: Understanding trajectories
Difficulty: 2
No. of players: Groups of 5-6
Material: One ball and one goalmouth per group
Description: Player A throws the ball over the goal to B who heads the ball on the goal defended by C.

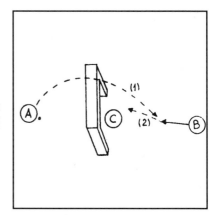

Objective: Understanding trajectories
Difficulty: 3
No. of players: Groups of 5-6
Material: 4-5 balls per group and a goalmouth
Description: Diagram indicates player's positions. Player A sends the ball with different trajectories over the goal for player B to shoot on goal with a header. Players exchange positions.

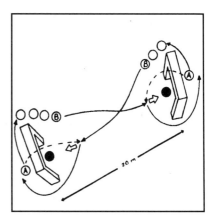

Objective: Understanding trajectories
Difficulty: 3
No. of players: Groups of 5-6
Material: 4-5 balls per group and one player
Description: Diagram indicates players' positions. Player A sends a ball with different trajectories for B to shoot on goal with a header. Exercise is done on the other side by C and D.

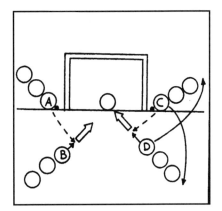

Objective: Understanding trajectories
Difficulty: 2
No. of players: Groups of 5-6
Material: 4-5 balls per group and a goalmouth
Description: Player A, positioned in the goalmouth as a goalie, throws the ball with different trajectories to B who runs and jumps to head the ball on goal.

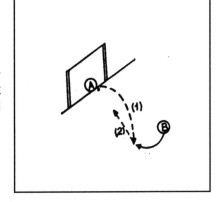

Objective: Understanding trajectories
Difficulty: 2
No. of players: Groups of 4
Material: One ball and two goalmouths per group
Description: Two players are positioned within each goalmouth, face to face, 5 yards apart. Both teams shoot at the other goal with headers. The players can head the ball first time from the shot or settle and pass the ball in the air for their teammate to head.

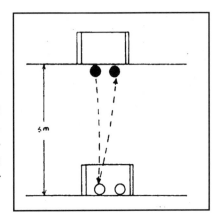

Objective: Understanding trajectories
Difficulty: 3
No. of players: Groups of 5-6
Material: 4-5 balls and a goalmouth per group
Description: Player A sends the ball to his team-mate B who tries to score with a header in the goal defended by C.

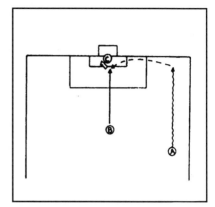

Objective: Understanding trajectories
Difficulty: 4
No. of players: Groups of 5-6
Material: 4-5 balls and one goalmouth per group
Description: Player A dribbles and crosses for B who heads to C to shoot on goal with a header.

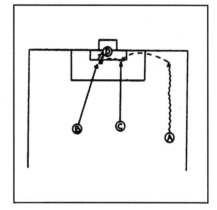

Objective: Understanding trajectories
Difficulty: 4
No. of players: Groups of 5-6
Material: 4-5 balls per group and one goal-mouth
Description: Player A dribbles and crosses for C who flicks to B to shoot on goal with a header.

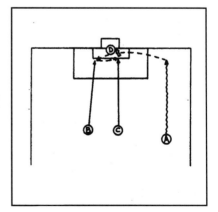

Objective: Understanding trajectories
Difficulty: 3
No. of players: Groups of 5-6
Material: 4-5 balls per group and a goal-mouth
Description: Player A dribbles and crosses for B who shoots on goal with a header.

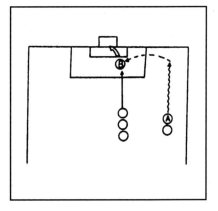

Objective: Understanding trajectories
Difficulty: 4
No. of players: Groups of 5-6
Material: 4-5 balls per group
Description: Player A makes a long air pass to B who heads the ball to C who receives and dribbles to A's position. After the exercise they exchange positions.

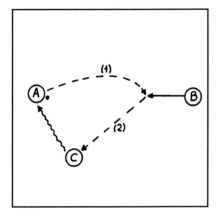

Heading with a body turn

Objective: Heading with a body turn
Difficulty: 2
No. of players: Groups of 2
Material: One ball per group
Description: Player B goes to the right or to the left and his teammate A sends the ball for B to head back.

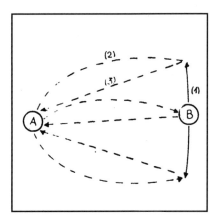

Objective: Heading with a body turn
Difficulty: 2
No. of players: Groups of 2
Material: One ball per group
Description: This exercise is similar to the previous one except that player A decides the direction of the pass and B must react quickly.

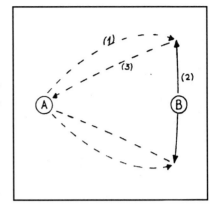

Objective: Heading with a body turn
Difficulty: 2
No. of players: Groups of 5 to 8
Material: One ball per player
Description: Player A heads each ball passed to him back to the passer, moving from B to C to D to E and so on.

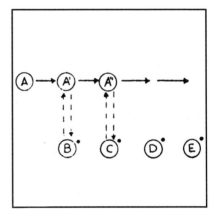

Objective: Heading with a body turn
Difficulty: 4
No. of players: Groups of 2
Material: One ball per group
Description: Players A and B pass the ball back and forth with their heads while running toward the goal.

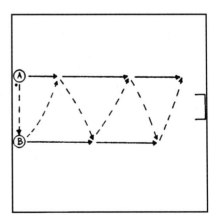

Objective: Heading with a body turn
Difficulty: 2
No. of players: Groups of 4
Material: One ball per group
Description: Player A serves the ball to his team-mate B who shoots on the goal defended by the opposing pair. C and D then repeat the exercise.

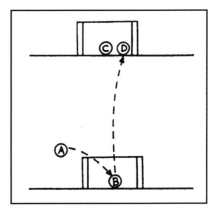

Objective: Heading with a body turn
Difficulty: 3
No. of players: Groups of 6-10
Material: One ball per group
Description: Players are positioned in a triangular formation and pass the ball to each other with their heads. A to C to B to C to A to C and so on.

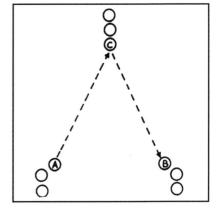

Objective: Heading with a body turn
Difficulty: 3
No. of players: Groups of 4-8
Material: One ball per group
Description: Player B passes to A and moves rapidly to the right or to the left to head the return pass from A.

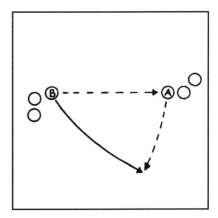

Objective: Heading with a body turn
Difficulty: 4
No. of players: Groups of 4 or 5
Material: One ball per group
Description: Player A is positioned in the center of a circle formed by 4 or 5 players who make revolutions around him. A passes the ball to one of the outside players who returns it to him with a header.

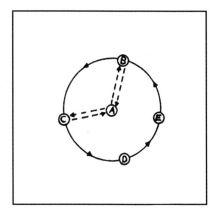

Objective: Heading with a body turn
Difficulty: 3
No. of players: Groups of 3
Material: One ball per group
Description: Players A, B and C are positioned in a triangular formation. B and C run forward while A runs backward. Passing order is as follows: A to C to B to A and so on.

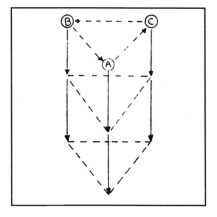

Objective: Heading with a body turn
Difficulty: 3
No. of players: Groups of 4 or 5
Material: One ball per group
Description: Player A runs in a straight line to receive the ball sent by B and passes it with his head to C.

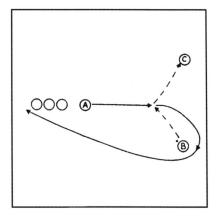

Objective: Heading with a body turn
Difficulty: 3
No. of players: Groups of 8 to 10
Material: One ball per group
Description: Player A runs in a straight line and receives passes from B, C and D to head them to their respective teammates 1, 2, and 3.

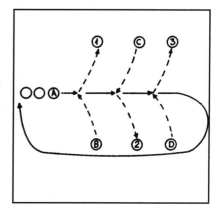

Objective: Heading with a body turn
Difficulty: 4
No. of players: Groups of 4 or 5
Material: One ball per group
Description: Player A is located within a circle formed by 4 or 5 players. All play with the head. B passes the ball to A who passes to C who returns it to him to repeat with D, etc.

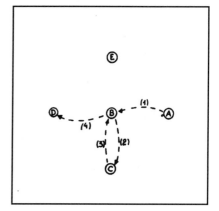

Objective: Heading with a body turn
Difficulty: 3
No. of players: Groups of 2
Material: One ball and 6 bowling pins per pair
Description: Player A sends the ball to B who heads the ball to knock down as many pins as possible.

Flick-on headers

Objective: Flick-on headers
Difficulty: 3
No. of players: Groups of 3
Material: One ball per group
Description: Player A sends the ball to B who flicks it backward to C. C collects the ball and passes to B who flicks to A and so on.

Objective: Flick-on headers
Difficulty: 3
No. of players: Groups of 3
Material: One ball per group
Description: Player A sends the ball to B who flicks it backward to C; C heads it first time back to B and so on.

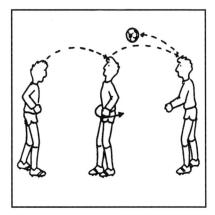

Objective: Flick-on headers
Difficulty: 3
No. of players: Various groups
Material: Two balls per group
Description: Player A sends the ball to E who flicks it on to C. Immediately he turns toward B who passes to him and he flicks on to D and so on.

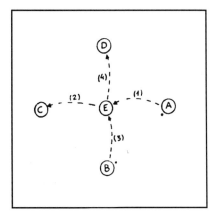

Objective: Flick-on headers
Difficulty: 3
No. of players: Various groups
Material: One ball per group
Description: The players are positioned in a line and pass the ball among them by means backward flick-on headers. The last player in line (player B) restarts the exercise in the opposite direction.

Objective: Flick-on headers
Difficulty: 3
No. of players: Groups of 4
Material: One ball per group
Description: Player A passes the ball to B who heads the ball backward to D; at this time all the players turn and C receives the pass from D and heads the ball backward to A and so on.

Objective: Flick-on headers
Difficulty: 3
No. of players: Groups of 3
Material: One ball per group
Description: The players are in a row and play backward headers to the next in line; after passing, the player moves to the back of the line.

Objective: Flick-on headers
Difficulty: 3
No. of players: Groups of 5
Material: One ball per group
Description: Player A passes the ball to Y who flicks on to the next Y with a header in spite of the opposition of defender X.

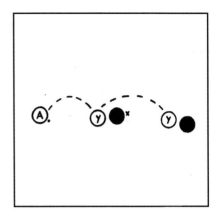

Objective: Flick-on headers
Difficulty: 3
No. of players: Groups of 3
Material: One ball and two cones per group
Description: Player A throws the ball to his teammate B who heads the ball backward in spite of the opposition of defender C.

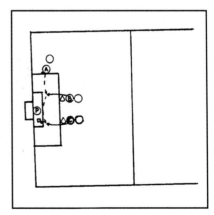

Objective: Flick-on headers
Difficulty: 3
No. of players: Various groups
Material: One ball and two cones per group
Description: Player A crosses a ball into the goalmouth to B who is coming in from outside of the area; B flicks on a header backwards to C who shoots on goal.

Objective: Flick-on headers
Difficulty: 3
No. of players: Various groups
Material: One ball and two cones per group
Description: Player A crosses a ball into the goalmouth to B who is coming in from the goal line area; B flicks on a header backwards to C who shoots on goal.

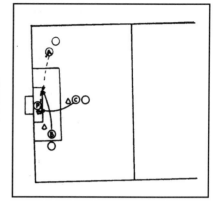

Objective: Flick-on headers
Difficulty: 3
No. of players: Various groups
Material: One ball and two cones per group
Description: Player A crosses a ball into the goalmouth to teammates B and C who are coming in from the goal line; B or C flicks the ball backward with his head for D who shoots on goal.

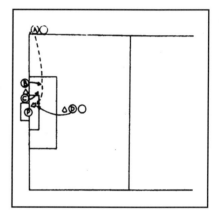

Heading with opponents present

Objective: Heading with opponents present
Difficulty: 3
No. of players: Groups of 8-10
Material: One ball per group
Description: Two teams positioned in two parallel rows attempt to head the ball thrown by A. The team that manages to head the ball over the opposing line gets a point.

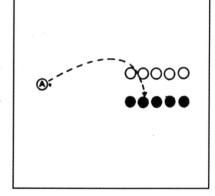

Objective: Heading with opponents present
Difficulty: 2
No. of players: Groups of 5-6
Material: One ball per group
Description: One player throws the ball consecutively to his teammates who are positioned in a line and return it to him with a header in spite of the opposition of the other two.

Objective: Heading with opponents present
Difficulty: 3
No. of players: Groups of 3
Material: One ball per group
Description: Player A throws the ball in the air so that B and C jump and attempt to score with their head in spite of the other's opposition.

Objective: Heading with opponents present
Difficulty: 3
No. of players: Groups of 3
Material: One ball per group
Description: Player A throws a ball toward players B and C who fight for it and head it back to A.

Objective: Heading with opponents present
Difficulty: 3
No. of players: Groups of 4
Material: One ball per group
Description: Player A throws to B who, in spite of C's opposition, heads the ball toward his teammate D.

Objective: Heading with opponents present
Difficulty: 3
No. of players: Groups of 3
Material: One ball per group
Description: Player B returns the ball sent by A with a header in spite of C's opposition; this exercise is done while moving forward.

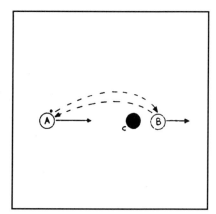

Objective: Heading with opponents present
Difficulty: 3
No. of players: Groups of 3
Material: One ball per group
Description: Player C moves to the right or the left to avoid B and return the pass from a with a header.

Objective: Heading with opponents present
Difficulty: 4
No. of players: Groups of 5
Material: One ball per group
Description: 2 v 2 fight for the ball thrown by player A using only head play. Each team defends its own goal and attacks the opponent's.

Objective: Heading with opponents present
Difficulty: 4
No. of players: Groups of 6-8
Material: One ball per group
Description: 3 v 3 + 2 goalies. Each team attempts to score in the opponent's goal using only head play. If the ball falls to the ground, possession switches to the other team's goalie who restarts with a throw.

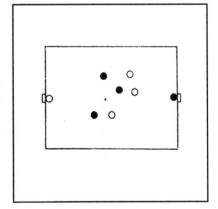

Objective: Heading with opponents present
Difficulty: 4
No. of players: Groups of 4
Material: One ball per group
Description: Player A crosses the ball toward the goalmouth where B attempts the shot in spite of the opposition of players X and Y.

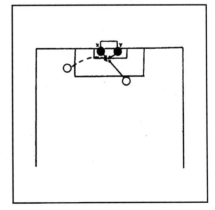

Objective: Heading with opponents present
Difficulty: 4
No. of players: Groups of 3
Material: One ball and two goals per group
Description: Player A throws a ball that is challenged for by B and C to head into the other's goal.

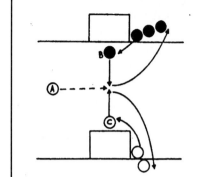

Objective: Heading with opponents present
Difficulty: 3
No. of players: Various groups
Material: 4-5 balls per group
Description: Player Y crosses into the goalmouth for his teammates who try to head on goal in spite of the opposition. The goal is defended by 4 players who must stand on the goal line and may only use their heads to stop the shot.

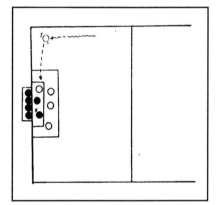

Objective: Heading with opponents present
Difficulty: 3
No. of players: Various groups
Material: 4-5 balls and two cones per group
Description: Team Y attacks the goal defended by team X. Y players outside the zone marked with cones cannot enter the zone, they can only send passes into the zone for their teammates to shoot on goal with headers.

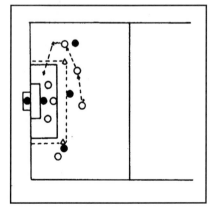

Objective: Heading with opponents present
Difficulty: 4
No of players: Various groups
Material: 4-5 balls and two cones per group
Description: Player Y crosses balls into the goal-mouth defended by team X. Players of team Y fight to try the shot on goal with a header. If in three tries the Y team can't get a shot on goal, the teams change roles.

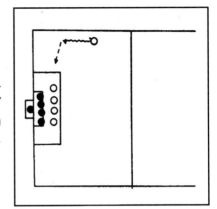

Objective: Heading with opponents present
Difficulty: 3
No. of players: Various groups
Material: 4 balls per group
Description: The diagram indicates the players' positions. The center players send the ball toward the outside where players X and Y fight to head the return pass to the inside player.

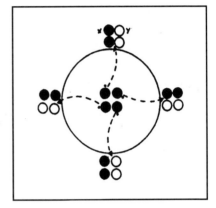

Objective: Heading with opponents present
Difficulty: 3
No. of players: Various groups
Material: One ball per group
Description: Player A passes the ball to B who dribbles and crosses into the goalmouth for his teammates C and D who criss-cross to avoid defender X's opposition.

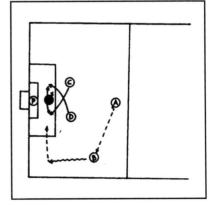

Objective: Heading with opponents present
Difficulty: 3
No. of players: Various groups
Material: One ball per group
Description: Player A throws the ball in the air for player B who, in spite of defender X's opposition, attempts the shot on goal with a header.

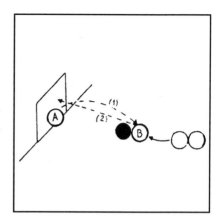

Objective: Heading with opponents present
Difficulty: 3
No. of players: Various groups
Material: One ball per group
Description: All the players within the circle try to keep the ball in the air with their heads. Each successful touch scores a point for that player's team.

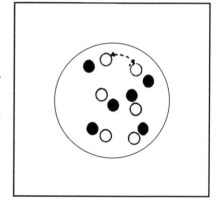

Objective: Opponents present
Difficulty: 3
No. of players: Various groups
Material: One ball and 4 cones per group
Description: Player A passes the ball to the inside of the grid where 4 players fight to attempt to head the ball to a teammate.

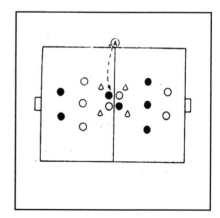

Diving header

Objective: Diving header
Difficulty: 2
No. of players: Groups of 2
Material: One ball per group
Description: Two kneeling players face each other; one player tosses a short ball to his partner that forces him to fall forward to head the ball back.

Objective: Diving header
Difficulty: 2
No. of players: Groups of 2
Material: One ball per group
Description: The standing player throws the ball to his teammate B who is kneeling. The throw must be short to force the kneeling player to fall forward to head the ball back.

Objective: Diving header
Difficulty: 2
No. of players: Groups of 2
Material: One ball per group
Description: The standing player A throws the ball to his teammate B who is squatting. The throw must be short to force player B to thrust himself forward to head the ball back.

Objective: Diving header
Difficulty: 3
No. of players: Groups of 2
Material: One ball per group
Description: Player A throws the ball to B who makes a diving header after the bounce.

Objective: Diving header
Difficulty: 3
No. of players: Groups of 2
Material: One ball per group
Description: Similar to the previous exercise except B makes a run up before diving to head the ball back to player A. Also, player B takes the ball in the air before the bounce.

Objective: Diving header
Difficulty: 3
No. of players: Groups of 2
Material: One ball and two cones per group
Description: Player A throws the ball to B who tries to get the ball by A with a diving header.

Objective: Diving header
Difficulty: 3
No. of players: Groups of 2
Material: One ball per group
Description: Player A sends a ball to B who with a diving header passes the ball to C. The exercise is repeated in the opposite direction.

Objective: Diving header
Difficulty: 3
No. of players: Groups of 2
Material: One ball, one bench and one mat per group
Description: Player A sends the ball to B who jumps over the bench to send a diving header back to A.

Objective: Diving header
Difficulty: 3
No. of players: Groups of 3
Material: One ball and two mats per group
Description: Player A is positioned between players B and C and makes alternate diving headers from the short throws made by B and C.

Objective: Diving header
Difficulty: 3
No. of players: Groups of 3
Material: One ball per group
Description: Player A passes the ball so that B
shoots with a diving header.

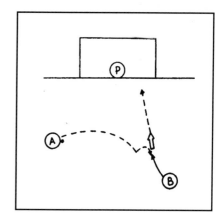

Application plays

Objective: Heading: Application plays
Difficulty: 3
No. of players: Groups of 8-10
Material: One ball and two boxes per group
Description: The two teams play only with the
head to put the ball inside the opposing team's
box.

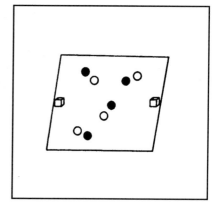

Objective: Heading: Application plays
Difficulty: 3
No. of players: Groups of 8-10
Material: One ball and two hoops per group
Description: Two teams of 4 stationary players
each defend a hoop. Each team attempts to put
the ball through the opposition's hoop using
only head play.

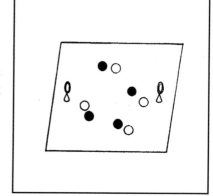

Objective: Heading: Application plays
Difficulty: 3
No. of players: Groups of 8-19
Material: One ball per group
Description: Two teams of 4-5 players try to score in the opposition's goal using only head play. The passes between teammates can be made with the hands.

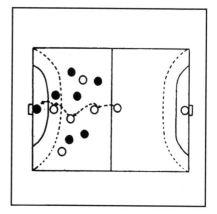

Objective: Heading: Application plays
Difficulty: 3
No. of players: Groups of 8-10
Material: One ball per group and volleyball rules
Description: Two teams play soccer volleyball using only head play. Each team has 3 head touches to send the ball to the opponent's side. If the opposing team cannot return it in three or less touches, one point is scored.

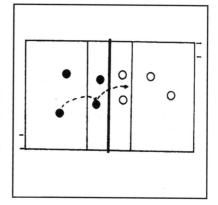

Objective: Heading: Application plays
Difficulty: 4
No. of players: Groups of 8-10
Material: One ball per group
Description: One team is positioned in the center zone and tries to intercept the passes of the opposing team who are positioned on either side. Head passes and head interceptions are required.

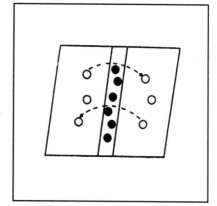

Objective: Heading: Application plays
Difficulty: 3
No. of players: Various groups
Material: Posts and volleyball net, and a ball
Description: Soccer-volleyball: players have three head touches to send the ball to the opposing field. The objective is for the ball to touch the ground on the opposition's side.

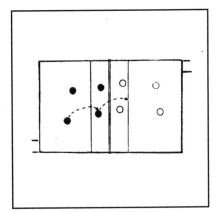

Objective: Heading: Application plays
Difficulty: 3
No. of players: Various groups
Material: Posts and tennis net, and a ball
Description: Soccer-tennis: players can play with heads and feet but can only head pass the ball to the opposition's field; the ball can only bounce once. Each team can make only three touches to pass the ball to the opposition's side.

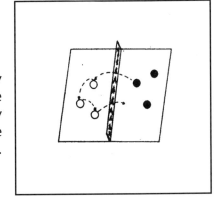

Objective: Heading: Application plays
Difficulty: 4
No. of players: Various groups
Material: 4-5 balls per group
Description: Player A crosses the ball into the goalmouth defended by a 5 player team who can't move from the goal line and can only use their heads to clear the opposition's shots. After 5 minutes roles are exchanged

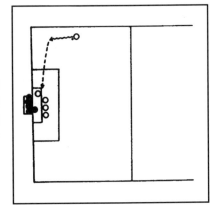

Objective: Heading: Application plays
Difficulty: 3
No. of players: Various groups
Material: One ball per group
Description: Two teams vie for possession of the ball with their heads. Before passing the ball to a teammate, each player must make a prior touch with the head.

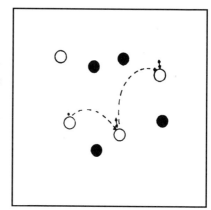

Objective: Heading: Application plays
Difficulty: 3
No. of players: Various groups
Material: One ball per group
Description: A 3 player team attempts to score on P's goal using only head play. Defender X attempts to prevent the three attackers from shooting.

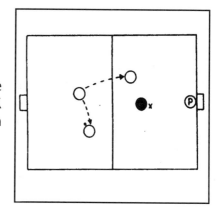

Objective: Heading: Application plays
Difficulty: 3
No. of players: Various groups
Material: One ball per group
Description: 2 v 2 using only head play. Each team tries to invade the opposition's goal-mouth.

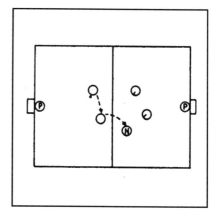

CHAPTER 8

COMPLEMENTARY ACTIVITIES
Application plays for soccer

Objective: Soccer: Application plays
Difficulty: 3
No. of players: Various groups
Material: One ball per group
Description: Two teams are divided into two groups and are positioned in two zones. No player may leave his area. Both groups must attack the same goals.

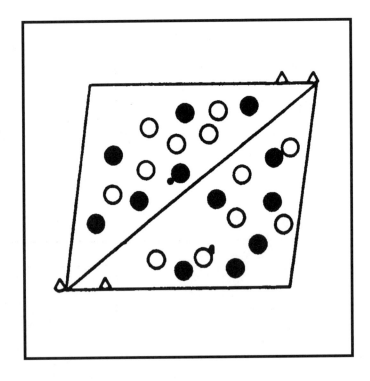

Objective: Soccer: Application plays
Difficulty: 3
No. of players: Various groups
Material: One ball per group
Description: 6 v 6 on a reduced area where the goals are located within the field of play. The play can be developed on either side of the goals.

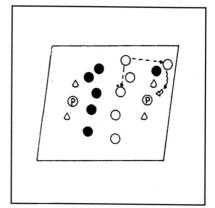

Objective: Soccer: Application plays
Difficulty: 3
No. of players: Various groups
Material: One ball per group
Description: Four teams with 4 players and 4 goals. Each team defends its own goal and attacks any of the other three.

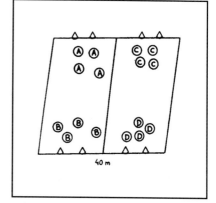

Objective: Soccer - Application plays
Difficulty: 3
No. of players: Various groups
Material: One ball and 10 cones per group
Description: Players are divided into 3 groups of an irregular number because each one defends goals of different sizes. Each team defends its own goal and can attack any of the others.

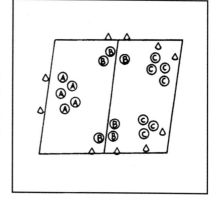

Objective: Soccer: Application plays
Difficulty: 3
No. of players: Various groups
Material: One ball and 6 cones per group
Description: The diagram indicates the position of the players. The team composed of six players must simultaneously play against the two teams of four. They defend one goal and attack two.

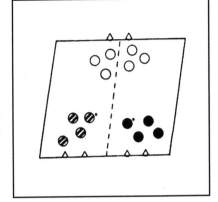

Objective: Soccer: Application plays
Difficulty: 3
No. of players: Various groups
Material: One ball and 8 cones per group
Description: The diagram indicates the position of the players. Team A can score in goals 3 and 4. Team C can score in goals 1 and 2; team B scores a point each time they put a ball on the lines between goals 1-2 and 3-4.

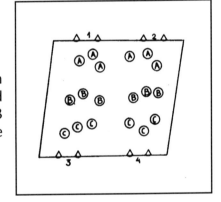

Objective: Soccer: Application plays
Difficulty: 3
No. of players: Various groups
Material: One ball and 8 cones per group
Description: The diagram indicates the position of the players. A v B: A defends goals 1-2, and attacks goals 3-4. Team B defends 3-4 and attacks 1-2. At the same time C v D: D attacks goals 1-2 and defends 3-4, while C attacks 3-4 and defends 1-2.

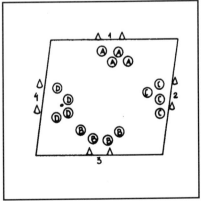

Objective: Soccer: Application plays
Difficulty: 3
No. of players: Various groups
Material: One ball and 8 cones per group
Description: The diagram indicates the position of the players. Each team must defend and attack two goals

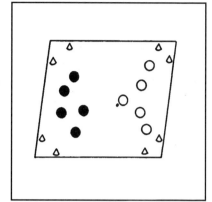

Objective: Soccer: Application plays
Difficulty: 3
No. of players: Various groups
Material: One ball and 6 cones per group
Description: The diagram indicates the position of the players. Each team defends their own goal and must attack the goal of the team located to their right.

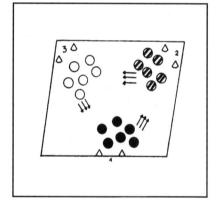

Objective: Soccer: Application plays
Difficulty: 3
No. of players: Various groups
Material: One ball and 4 cones per group
Description: Team X v Team Y within X's defensive zone ; if the defenders X win possession of the ball, they must attempt to cross the midfield line to face Team Z; players Y can fight to get back the ball until the X players cross the midfield line. If Team Y manages to keep the ball and scores a goal, Team X again is on the defense, and Team Y attacks Team Z.

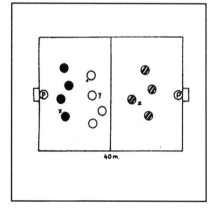

Objective: Soccer: Application plays
Difficulty: 3
No. of players: Various groups
Material: One ball per group
Description: The diagram indicates the position of the players. Team X defends a regulation goal against Team Y who defends two small goals.

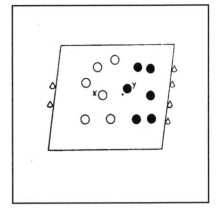

Objective: Soccer: Application plays
Difficulty: 3
No. of players: Various groups
Material: One ball and 4 cones per group
Description: Team X, who defends the regulation goal, must attack the two small goals defended by Team Y. If Team Y wins the ball within its defensive zone, marked by a dotted line, they must counterattack quickly to the regulation goal; if they win the ball outside of their defensive zone, they attack the small goals.

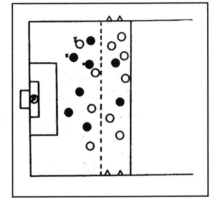

Objective: Soccer: Application plays
Difficulty: 3
No. of players: Various groups
Material: One ball and 4 cones per group
Description: Two teams face off in a playing field with barricades. The barricades can be used as walls to overtake the opposing defenders.

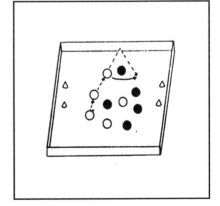

Objective: Soccer: Application plays
Difficulty: 3
No. of players: Various groups
Material: One ball and 8 cones per group
Description: Two teams defend three goals and attack the other three. The team with fewer goals after a predetermined time gives up their place to the Z team.

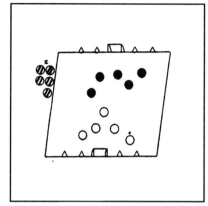

Objective: Soccer: Application plays
Difficulty: 3
No. of players: Various groups
Material: One ball per group
Description: One team of 6 players, defending a large goal, attacks a small goal defended by 3 defenders. Each team has 60 seconds to score.

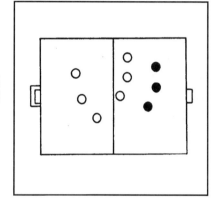

Objective: Soccer: Application plays
Difficulty: 3
No. of players: Various groups
Material: One ball per group
Description: 6 v 6 on a handball field. Goals from inside the area must be scored with the head, while from outside they can be scored in any way.

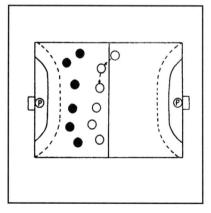

Objective: Soccer: Application plays
Difficulty: 3
No. of players: Various groups
Material: One ball and several boxes per group
Description: 6 v 6 on a reduced field. The objective is to put the greater number of balls inside the boxes; the passes can made with the feet, but the ball must be put in the boxes with the head.

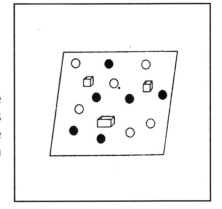

Objective: Soccer: Application plays
Difficulty: 3
No. of players: Various groups
Material: One ball per group
Description: 6 v 6 on a reduced field. The objective is to put the greater number of balls inside the zones located in the corners.

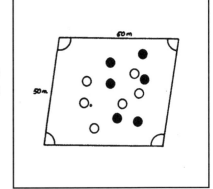

Objective: Soccer: Application plays
Difficulty: 3
No. of players: Various groups
Material: One ball per group
Description: On a reduced field, 6 v 6 + a neutral player who plays with the team in possession. The objective is to score a goal but only with a first touch (center volley, center head, etc.).

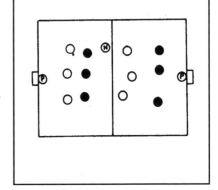

Application plays for offensive soccer

Objective: Application plays - offensive soccer
Difficulty: 3
No. of players: Various groups
Material: One ball per group
Description: Two offensive players with a neutral player in midfield face off against two defenders; the outside player can't join the attack, he may only serve as support player.

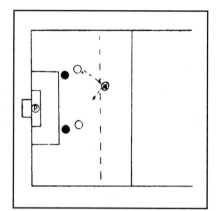

Objective: Application plays - offensive soccer
Difficulty: 3
No. of players: Various groups
Material: One ball per group
Description: 3 offensive + 2 support players v 3 defenders; the support players can't pass the line that determines their limited area. From their position they can contribute to the attack with deep passes, supports, etc. The 3 offensive players try to invade P's goalmouth.

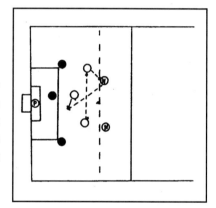

Objective: Application plays - offensive soccer
Difficulty: 3
No. of players: Numerous players
Material: One ball per group
Description: 3 offensive + 2 support players in midfield v 3 defensive + 1 support player in the midfield; the support players can't pass the line that determines their limited area. From their location they can contribute to the attack with deep passes, supports, etc. in spite of the opposition of the defender who also must stay in midfield. The 3 attackers attempt to invade P's goalmouth.

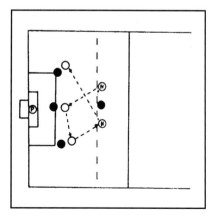

Objective: Application plays - offensive soccer
Difficulty: 3
No. of players: Various groups
Material: One ball per group
Description: 2 offensive + 2 support players in midfield v 2 defenders; the attackers attempt to play 2 v 2 with their markers and use their support when needed; the support players can't enter the offensive zone, except when the ball is in their zone and one of them thrusts forward to the attack so that his teammate makes a deep pass to him.

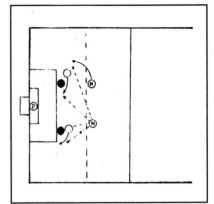

Objective: Application plays - offensive soccer
Difficulty: 3
No. of players: Various groups
Material: One ball per group
Description: The diagram indicates 2 offensive with 2 support players in midfield v 3 defenders + 1 support player in midfield. The offensive support players play with their teammates on either side with passes and can only cross into the offensive zone by dribbling the ball; the defensive support player cannot move into the attacking zone under any circumstance. When an attacking support player dribbles into the zone, he is challenged by the free defender and a 3 v 3 develops.

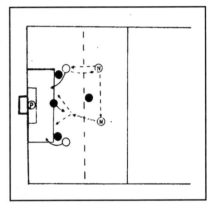

Objective: Application plays - offensive soccer
Difficulty: 3
No. of players: Various groups
Material: One ball per group
Description: 6 v 6 + 2 neutral players in midfield who pass the ball from the defense to the offense. In each defensive zone they play a 3 v 3. When the defense wins the ball, they must look to pass to the neutral player in midfield, in spite of the opposition from the 3 offensive players who try to regain possession of the ball; if the ball gets to midfield, the neutral player passes back to the defenders and they become the attackers.

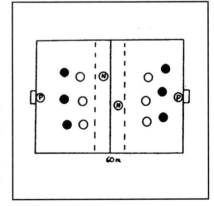

Objective: Application plays - offensive soccer
Difficulty: 4
No. of players: Various groups
Material: One ball per group
Description: The diagram indicates the position of 6 attackers v 7 defenders.
The offensive midfielders must act as support players and only one is allowed to dribble into the offensive zone or receive a deep pass; if he does not participate in the action when he enters the offensive zone, he must return to the midfield zone.

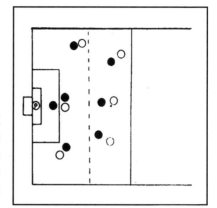

Objective: Application plays - offensive soccer
Difficulty: 4
No. of players: Various groups
Material: One ball per group
Description: The diagram indicates the location of 6 attackers v 5 defenders. The 3 forward attackers try to score in P's goal. Only one of the offensive support players can move into the offensive zone, but only when the ball gets to zones A or B.

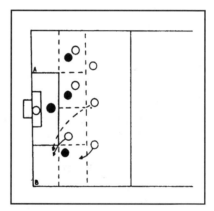

Objective: Application plays - offensive soccer
Difficulty: 4
No. of players: Various groups
Material: One ball per group
Description: 11 v 11 on a regulation field; each team has 45 seconds to score.

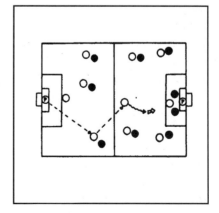

Objective: Application plays: offensive soccer
Difficulty: 4
No. of players: Various groups
Material: 1 ball per group
Description: 8 attackers v 8 defenders, and in the center of the field two neutral players whose function is to pass the ball from the defense to the offense. In each zone 4 v 4 is played and when the defense wins possession, they must get the ball to the players in the center of the field in spite of the opposition from the 4 offensive players who try to regain possession of the ball. If the ball gets to the center of the field, the neutral player passes back to the defenders who turn and become the attackers.

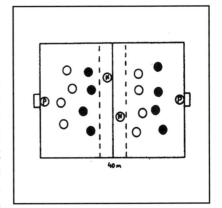

Small-sided games

Objective: Small-sided games
Difficulty: 3
No. of players: Various groups
Material: One ball per group
Description: In several small areas marked on the field, different games of 5 v 2 are played.

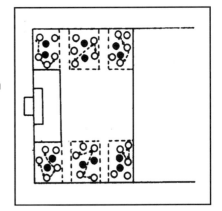

Objective: Small-sided games
Difficulty: 3
No. of players: Various groups
Material: One ball per group
Description: Half the field is divided to carry out different games. On the corners 5 v 2, 4 v 4 in the penalty area, and between the area and the center of the field 6 v 6. Every so often the groups are rotated.

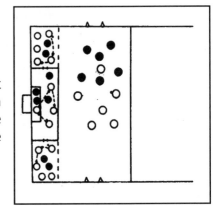

Objective: Small-sided games
Difficulty: 3
No. of players: Various groups
Material: One ball per group
Description: In several small areas marked on the field, different games of 3 v 3 are played.

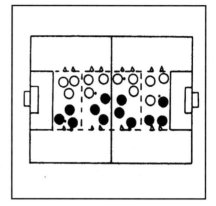

Objective: Small-sided games
Difficulty: 3
No. of players: Various groups
Material: One ball per group
Description: In several small areas marked on the field, different games of 2 v 2 are played.

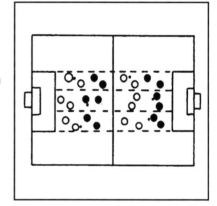

Objective: Small-sided games
Difficulty: 3
No. of players: Various groups
Material: One ball and 4 cones per group
Description: In a small area, two teams of 4 players attempt to invade the rival goalmouth. A goal can be scored through either side of the goal.

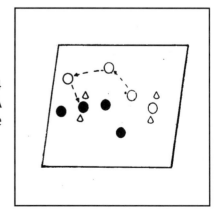

Objective: Small-sided games
Difficulty: 3
No. of players: Various groups
Material: One ball and 4 cones per group
Description: In a small area, two teams of 3 players each try to touch the cones with the ball. Each time a cone is touched the team wins one point.

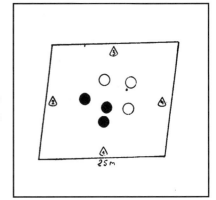

Objective: Small-sided games
Difficulty: 3
No. of players: Various groups
Material: One ball and 4 benches per group
Description: In a small area, two teams of 4 players try to score in the opposition's goal. The goal is the two benches plus the actual goal-mouth; if the ball touches a bench it is worth a point and if the ball enters the goal it is worth two points. One player from each team acts as goalie and attempts to defend the benches and the goal.

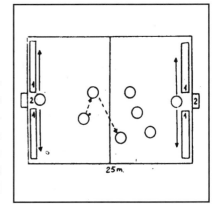

Objective: Small-sided games
Difficulty: 3
No. of players: Various groups
Material: One ball and 4 benches per group
Description: In a small area, two teams of 5 players try to score in the opposing goal. Games are to 2 and the reserve team takes the place of the losing team.

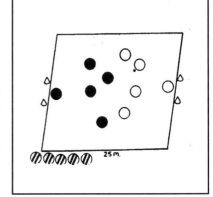

Objective: Small-sided games
Difficulty: 3
No. of players: Various groups
Material: One ball and 4 cones per groups
Description: In a small area, two teams of 3 players try to score in the opposing goal. After each goal, the teams switch sides.

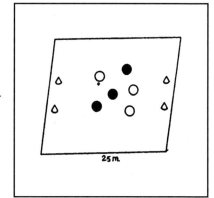

Objective: Small plays
Difficulty: 3
No. of players: Various groups
Material: One ball and different material per group
Description: In a small area, two teams of 3 players try to score in the opposing goal. Throughout the field are various obstacles that the players must navigate to invade the opposing goalmouth.

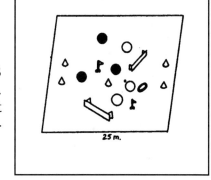

REEDSWAIN BOOKS

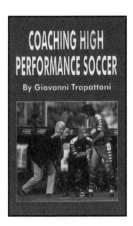

**Coaching High
Performance Soccer**
by Giovanni Trapattoni
#242: $12.95

Coaching Team Shape
by Emilio Cecchini
#243: $12.95

**Soccer Practice Plans
for Effective Training**
by Kenneth Sherry
#290: $14.95

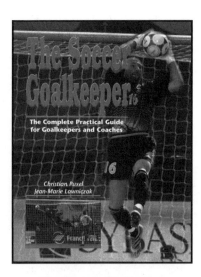

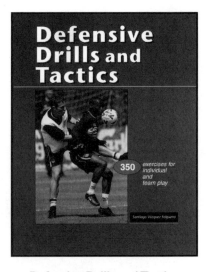

The Soccer Goalkeeper
**The Complete Practical Guide for
Goalkeepers and Coaches**
#160: $14.95

**Defensive Drills and Tactics
350 Exercises for Individual
and Team Play**
*by Santiago Vazquez Folgueira,
Barcelona FC*
#780: $14.95

1-800-331-5191 • www.reedswain.com

REEDSWAIN BOOKS

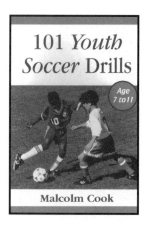

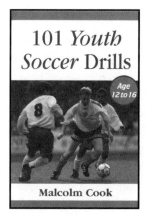

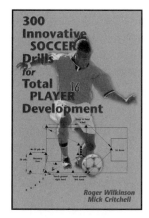

**101 Youth Soccer Drills
Ages 7-11**
by Malcolm Cook
#254: $14.95

**101 Youth Soccer Drills
Ages 12-16**
by Malcolm Cook
#255: $14.95

**300 Innovative
SOCCER DRILLS
for Total PLAYER
Development**
*by Roger Wilkinson
and Mick Critchell*
#188: $14.95

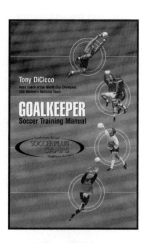

**24 Easy to Follow
Training Sessions
for 5-7 Year Olds**
by Peter Schreiner
#266: $12.95

**24 Easy to Follow
Practice Sessions
for 8-11 Year Olds**
by Peter Schreiner
#297: $12.95

**Tony DiCicco
Goalkeeper Training
Manual**
Edited by Mick Darcy
#164: $12.95

1-800-331-5191 • www.reedswain.com

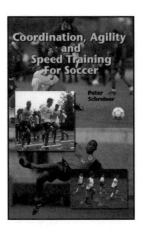

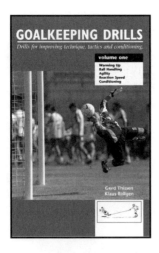

REEDSWAIN BOOKS

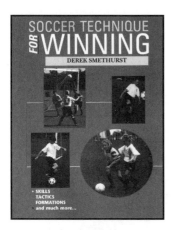

**Soccer Technique
for Winning**
by Derek Smethurst
#155: $14.95

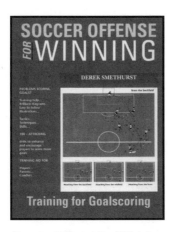

Soccer Offense for Winning
by Derek Smethurst
#156: $14.95

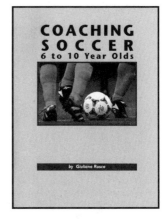

**Coaching Soccer
6 to 10 year Olds**
by Giuliano Rusca
#264: $14.95

**Soccer Training Games,
Drills, and Fitness Exercises**
by Malcolm Cook
#167: $14.95

**SOCCER TACTICS
An Analysis of Attack
and Defense**
by Massimo Lucchesi
#149: $12.95

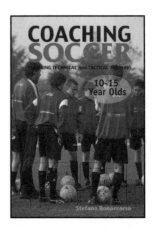

**Coaching Soccer
10-15 Year Olds**
by Stephano Bonaccorso
#782: $14.95

1-800-331-5191 • www.reedswain.com

REEDSWAIN BOOKS

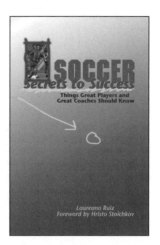
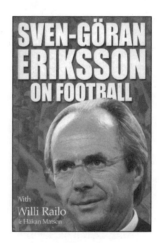

NOTES

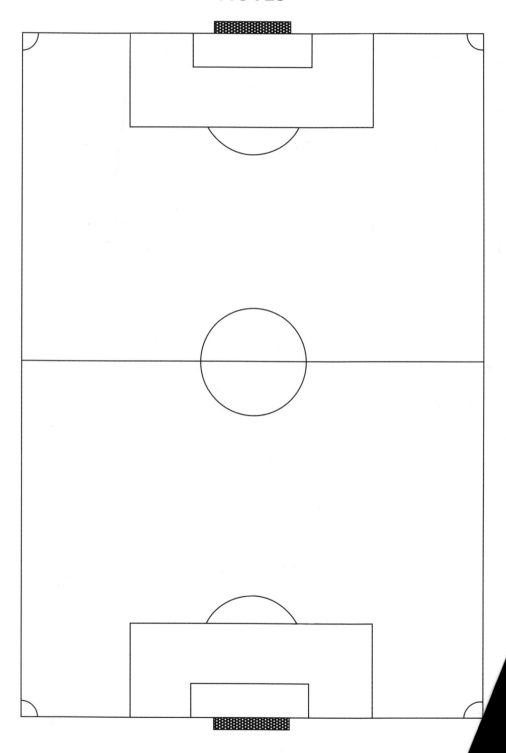

NOTES

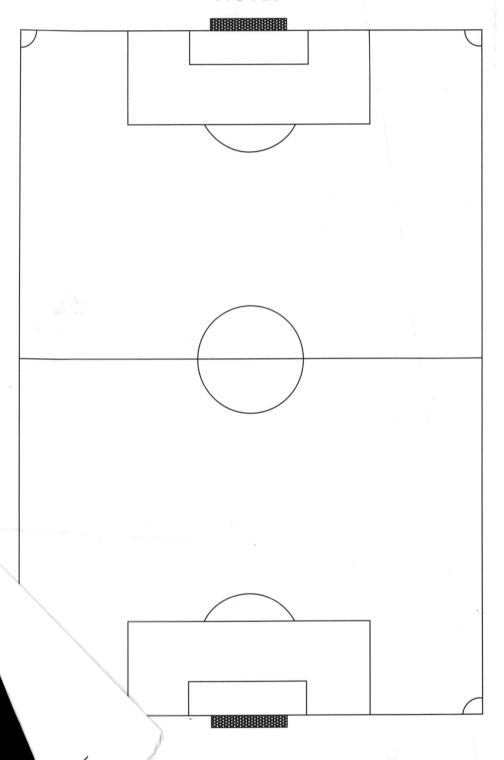

NOTES

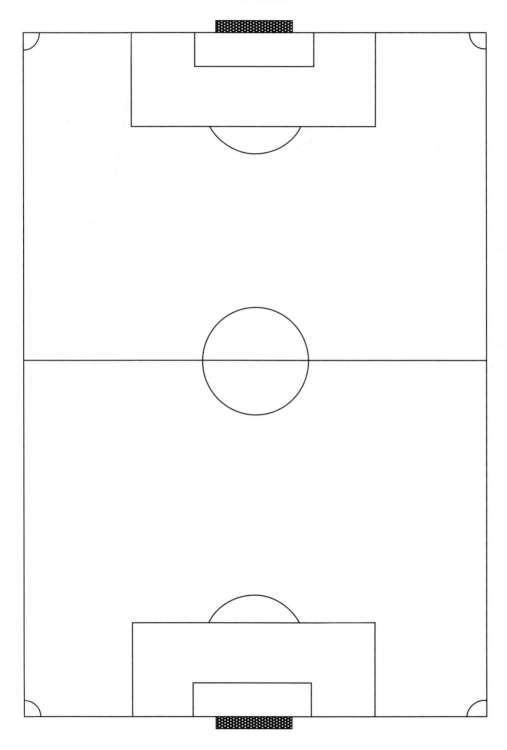

NOTES

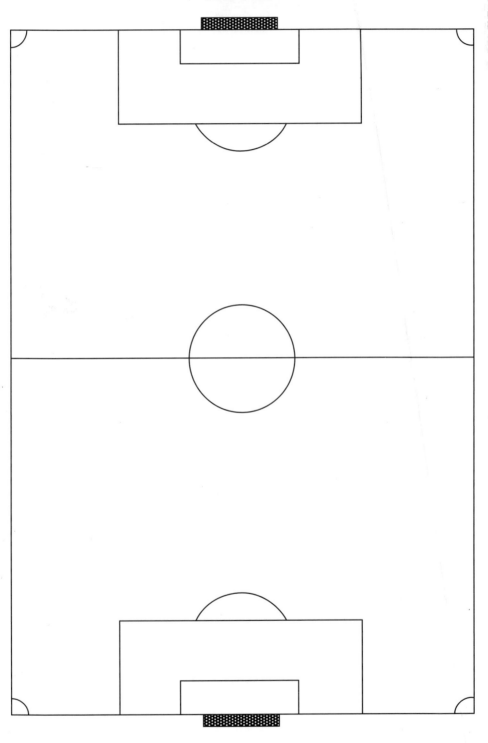

1-800-331-5191 • www.reedswain.com